CRAFTING
SEITAN

CREATING HOMEMADE PLANT-BASED MEATS

Skye Michael Conroy

BPC

Summertown, Tennessee

Library of Congress Cataloging-in-Publication Data

Names: Conroy, Skye Michael, author.

Title: Crafting seitan : creating homemade plant-based meats / Skye Michael Conroy.

Description: Summertown, TN : BPC, [2021] | Includes index. | Summary: "Chef Skye Michael Conroy offers delicious recipes for alternatives to commercially prepared and processed plant-based meat substitutes. Many of the flavors, appearances, and textures of meat dishes can be replicated from a home kitchen. Crafting Seitan offers step-by-step guidance for preparing more than 100 recipes using wheat-based seitan, soy products, and a variety of flavorings to create burgers, meatless meatballs, roasts, and every variety of shred, batter fry, skewer, steak, cutlet, chop, and barbecue under the sun. Also included are regional American favorites, as well as Asian, Mexican, and other international dishes. Chef Conroy shares his special tips and techniques for preparing a variety of shapes and textures. A special section of the book contains his personal spice blends and flavoring mixes, sauces and glazes, and even a few nondairy staples to enhance these delicious dishes"— Provided by publisher.

Identifiers: LCCN 2020044634 (print) | LCCN 2020044635 (ebook) | ISBN 9781570673962 | ISBN 9781570678080 (epub)

Subjects: LCSH: Vegan cooking. | Meat substitutes. | LCGFT: Cookbooks.

Classification: LCC TX837 .C5974 2021 (print) | LCC TX837 (ebook) | DDC 641.5/6362—dc23

LC record available at https://lccn.loc.gov/2020044634

LC ebook record available at https://lccn.loc.gov/2020044635

The Forest Stewardship Council® is an international nongovernmental organization that promotes environmentally appropriate, socially beneficial, and economically viable management of the world's forests. To learn more, visit www.fsc.org

Food photography/cover photo: Skye Michael Conroy
Stock photography: 123 RF
Cover and interior design: John Wincek

Printed in China

BPC
PO Box 99
Summertown, TN 38483
888-260-8458
bookpubco.com

ISBN: 978-1-57067-396-2

26 25 24   3 4 5 6 7 8 9

Disclaimer: The information in this book is presented for educational purposes only. It isn't intended to be a substitute for the medical advice of a physician, dietitian, or other health-care professional.

Contents

Acknowledgments

I wish to express my love and gratitude to my dearly departed friend Jean Bremner, who introduced me to vegetarianism many years ago; to my dear friend Suzy Bellew, who introduced me to veganism; to Josh Meckel, my computer technical expert, for his brilliant Gentle Chef website construction; to Louise Gagnon, my sous chef, confidante, and recipe tester; to my Gentle Chef Cooking Group administrators on Facebook: Kathryn Hill, Sandra Pope Hays, Martina Moore, Isabelle Nuenninghoff, and Michelle Harris Campoli; and to all of my readers for their continuing support and encouragement.

Compassion (derived from Latin and meaning "to suffer together with") is a profound human virtue and emotion prompted by the pain of other living beings and is ranked as one of the greatest virtues in numerous philosophies and spiritual traditions. More vigorous than empathy, the feeling of compassion commonly gives rise to an active desire to alleviate another's suffering.

Sentience implies the ability to experience pleasure and pain. As vegans, we believe that all sentient beings are entitled, at the very least, to the right not to be subjected to unnecessary suffering. This understanding of sentience and the desire to alleviate suffering is the primary motivator for embracing veganism and a strict plant-based diet.

For those who not only dream of a gentle and compassionate world but who also make the commitment to realize that dream, this book is dedicated to you.

Preface

Many people who embrace a plant-based diet do so for ethical reasons and not because they dislike the flavor and texture of meat. But finding satisfying meat alternatives is not always easy for individuals who once enjoyed the flavors and textures associated with meat-based dishes, or for individuals who grew up with meat-based dishes as a traditional part of their family or ethnic heritage.

This cookbook focuses on approximating the appearance, flavors, and textures of meat and the meat products that many of us grew up with: foods that are familiar, that represent our culture or heritage, and that evoke a feeling of nostalgia. Meat analogues provide the satisfaction of eating something we can sink our teeth into—hearty foods that fill us up and stick to our ribs, foods that remind us of holiday traditions, and foods that give rise to memories of cook-outs and camping trips with friends and family in the summertime.

My recipes may resemble meat too realistically for some people's taste; however, most people thrive on familiarity, and if that familiarity can be satisfied, there is a greater chance of success in maintaining a plant-based diet.

Seitan (seasoned and cooked gluten) is virtually unknown to most non-vegan Westerners, so name and appearance associations are very helpful in tempting people to try these new foods. I truly believe that most vegans are not looking for something entirely new; they're simply looking for the familiar done differently and compassionately.

You won't find nutrition information included with the recipes because the cookbook wasn't written for individuals monitoring calorie and nutrient intake. However, the recipes were created using wholesome ingredients as much as possible, and refined ingredients were included only when absolutely necessary to achieve proper textures.

In order to win people over to plant-based cuisine, my recipes were designed to offer the best flavors and textures. As a chef, I enjoy preparing comforting and satisfying meals. However, I also enjoy the health benefits of a well-balanced plant-based diet, and I encourage breaking the reliance on commercially prepared and heavily processed foods as much as possible.

Detailed instructions are included in the cookbook for preparing many of the components of my recipes with unprocessed, wholesome ingredients. My philosophy is "everything in moderation." Even plant-based foods can be unhealthy and fattening if they're not consumed sensibly.

Regarding food allergies and sensitivities: This cookbook relies on gluten and soy as the foundation for the meat analogue recipes. A few of the incidental recipes may be naturally gluten-free or soy-free, but that was not my intent when creating them. If you have a sensitivity to either gluten or soy, this cookbook isn't for you; instead, I recommend researching cookbooks and websites that are specifically geared for individuals with food sensitivities.

Creating superior-quality meat analogues at home is a complex art, and there is no doubt that I have many discoveries to make in the future. The recipes will continue to evolve as I continue to learn. I invite you to join me on my journey of discovery.

Chef Skye

Essential Tips
and Techniques

Special Ingredients

BEET POWDER is used in some of the meat analogues in this cookbook to provide the red color that would typically be produced by curing meats with nitrites and nitrates. Beet powder is not readily available but can be found in a few specialty food stores or purchased online. If you don't have beet powder in the pantry, the bright-red liquid from freshly cooked or canned beets (not pickled) can be used, but you'll have to experiment with producing the correct color intensity.

BROWNING LIQUID is used to create a rich brown color in soups, stews, and gravies. In meat analogues, especially those approximating beef, it is used as a color enhancer to produce a more appetizing appearance. Commercial versions, such as Gravy Master and Kitchen Bouquet, can be found in most grocery stores in the aisle where jarred gravy is located.

LIQUID SMOKE is a water-based seasoning distilled from real wood smoke; it is often used in meat analogues to provide a "cold-smoked" flavor. Some people are sensitive to smoke flavors or don't care for them at all, so you can omit it if you prefer. Liquid smoke can be found in most major grocery stores, usually in the aisle with condiments and marinades.

MELLOW WHITE MISO is used as a seasoning in many of the meat analogues in this cookbook. Miso adds umami (a Japanese word used to describe a pleasant savory flavor) to foods. Mellow white miso can be found in natural food stores in the refrigerated section. It has a very long shelf life (about two years), but it must be stored in the refrigerator. Yellow miso can also be used. If white or yellow miso is unavailable, you can replace it with 1 teaspoon nutritional yeast flakes plus 1 teaspoon tamari for every tablespoon of white miso called for in the meat analogue recipes.

MUSHROOM POWDER is used to add umami (a complex savory flavor) as well as color to many of the recipes in this book. It's an instant way to add an incredible depth of earthy flavor to hearty soups and stews, brown gravies, and sauces. Mushroom powder is available in many specialty and gourmet food markets and through online retailers. Alternatively, it can easily be prepared by grinding dried porcini, portobello, or shiitake mushrooms in a dry blender, spice grinder, or coffee grinder.

POULTRY SEASONING is a blend of aromatic herbs and spices and is commonly used, as the name implies, for seasoning poultry. For our purposes it is used as a flavoring ingredient in Chikun (page 14) and Turky (page 120) and their respective simmering broths. It can also be used to season stuffing or dressing, broths, soups, stews, gravies, and sauces. Poultry seasoning can be easily prepared at home using my own seasoning blend called Aromatica (page 161).

RED MISO has a deep brick-red color and a stronger flavor than white or yellow miso. It is used as a seasoning and coloring ingredient in Garden Ham (page 115) and Hard Salami (page 157). Red miso is available in natural food stores in the refrigerated section. It has a very long shelf life (about 2 years) but must be stored in the refrigerator. If red miso is unavailable, substitutions are offered in the recipes.

TEXTURED VEGETABLE/SOY PROTEIN GRANULES is a term used to describe a commercially produced soy-based meat analogue that is dried and packaged. Often abbreviated as TVP® and TSP, these products may be used interchangeably. Look for them in natural food stores, some larger supermarkets, and online.

Mise en Place

Mise en place (pronounced *meez-ahn-plahs*) is a French term (literally translated as "put in place") that refers to the assembly and preparation of all ingredients and tools before cooking begins. It is an important culinary technique but is most often ignored. Mise en place means that all ingredients should be cleaned, peeled, chopped, or measured beforehand.

Be sure to read and reread the recipes and other information in this cookbook prior to proceeding with the recipes. Many people prepare and cook at the same time, or simply don't read instructions carefully. These are bad habits that often lead to mistakes and failures. Practice mise en place consistently, and your cooking experience will be both a pleasure and a success.

Introduction to Meat Analogues

Meat analogues, or imitations, are generally understood within the vegan context to mean 100 percent plant-based foods that mimic or approximate certain aesthetic qualities (such as the texture, flavor, and appearance) of specific types of meat. This differs from meat substitutes or alternatives. For example, a grilled piece of tofu can serve as a substitute or alternative to meat, but when it's used as an ingredient and transformed in some way to replicate the texture of chicken or pork, it becomes a meat analogue.

Many modern commercial meat analogues are made from textured wheat protein (derived from gluten) and isolated soy protein, and these products closely approximate the texture of real meat. Plant proteins, in general, can be textured to mimic the properties of real meat (chicken, beef, or pork) using different factory processes, such as spinning, jet cooking, steam treatment, and extrusion cooking. Among these processes, extrusion has been the preferred technology.

However, for many people, including me, commercial meat analogues are often not satisfying, whether due to inaccurate flavor, appearance, and/or texture; the inclusion of too many refined and processed ingredients; or simply the lack of availability. Commercially prepared meat analogues can be expensive, too, and are not an affordable means of maintaining a well-balanced and nutritious plant-based diet on a day-to-day basis.

Some people may think that preparing meat analogues at home is too complex and may feel intimidated by the process, especially when they're looking at a long list of ingredients, but don't let this be a concern. While having some plant-based cooking experience is helpful, I have put a lot of forethought into writing the recipes in order for even the novice cook to achieve success.

If you're a former meat aficionado, remember that we can only approximate the aesthetic qualities of meat with plant-based ingredients and home kitchen equipment. Since we're working with plant-based ingredients, and not real meat originating from different animals with different diets, there's only so much we can do to create distinctly separate and unique flavor profiles in the analogues.

In other words, don't expect the analogues to share the exact nuances of their meat counterparts. If you curb your expectation of creating exact reproductions, then these recipes should more than satisfy your desire for meat-like appearances, textures, and flavors . . . compassionately.

Seitan and Plant-Protein Blends

Seitan (pronounced *say-tan*), or wheat meat, is an amazingly versatile, protein-rich meat analogue made from vital wheat gluten. The word seitan is of Japanese origin and was coined in 1961 by George Ohsawa, a Japanese advocate of the macrobiotic diet.

Gluten (from the Latin *gluten*, meaning "glue") is a protein complex that appears in foods processed from wheat and related species, including barley and rye. In baking, small amounts of vital wheat gluten are often added to yeast bread recipes to improve the texture and elasticity of the dough.

Wheat gluten is not a complete protein in itself (lysine is the missing amino acid), which means that additional ingredients (such as tofu, tamari, nutritional yeast, or bean flour) must be added to complete its amino acid profile. Lysine can also easily be obtained by consuming other plant-protein sources in the daily diet.

In the commercial production of vital wheat gluten, a mixture of wheat flour and water is kneaded vigorously by machinery until the gluten forms into a mass. The water is removed by a screw press and an additional factory process for drying without denaturing the protein. The gluten is then air cooled and transported to a receiving container. In the final step, the collected gluten is sifted and milled to produce a uniform product.

For preparing meat analogues, high-quality vital wheat gluten is essential in order to develop the proper elasticity in the dough. Be sure it is labeled as having a minimum of 75 percent protein. Bargain and bulk gluten may be a lower quality and could contain a significant amount of starch. Excess starch will yield a bread-like texture in the finished analogue.

Vital wheat gluten can be measured by volume by spooning the gluten into a measuring cup and leveling off the top with a table knife. Alternatively, it can be measured by weight, which will be more accurate.

Unfortunately, some individuals cannot benefit from the nutrition and versatility of seitan due to gluten sensitivity or total intolerance (Celiac disease) and must obtain their protein from vegetables, legumes, and gluten-free grains, such as quinoa, amaranth, and buckwheat (which is actually not a grain but a seed).

Although some of the meat analogues in this cookbook are based entirely on gluten (seitan), others are prepared by combining gluten with tofu or textured vegetable/soy protein. Combining gluten and tofu together to create a meat analogue is not a new concept; however, the proportion of the ingredients and the seasonings and cooking methods are what make these meat analogues unique.

Cooking methods vary depending on the type of plant protein being used and the desired finished texture, flavor, and appearance. Through much experimentation, I was able to determine which methods and ingredients provide the best results for each type of meat analogue.

Preparing meat analogues at home is an art and science unto itself, much like the art and science of baking. Whether the recipe calls for a teaspoon, a tablespoon, or a cup (or a fraction thereof), always use level measurements for precision.

Since volume measurements for dry ingredients can sometimes be unreliable, I have included metric weight measurements for primary recipe ingredients, such as vital wheat gluten and tofu. Volume measurements for water used to prepare the meat analogues include both standard US measurements and metric. And please, no "eyeballing" volume measurements; that may work for some cooking techniques, but it doesn't work when preparing meat analogues.

The recipes provided in this cookbook were formulated to produce appetizing results and have been tested many times in my own kitchen. Therefore, experimenting with ratios of dry ingredient to liquid ingredient is not recommended, as this can upset the moisture balance and change the texture significantly enough to negatively affect the finished product.

Adjusting or substituting seasonings to suit your taste is to be expected, but avoid substituting primary functional ingredients or adding large amounts of unspecified extra ingredients, as this can also upset the moisture balance or change flavors and textures significantly enough to negatively affect results. In other words, be creative and have fun, but don't make too many changes and then wonder why something didn't turn out properly.

Depending on the desired texture of the finished product, kneading is utilized in varying degrees to develop the gluten and create meat-like textures. Gluten strands form as the *glutenin* and *gliadin* molecules cross-link to create a submicroscopic network. Kneading promotes this formation.

In most recipes, kneading can be done by hand, by using an electric stand mixer with a dough hook (this is ideal for people who have weakness or disability in their hands or wrists), or by using a food processor fitted with either a plastic dough blade or a standard metal chopping blade. Never use a blender for kneading dough!

Recipes that produce meat analogues with "shredded" or "pulled" textures require vigorous kneading in a food processor in order to sufficiently develop the gluten strands in the dough. The food processor can be fitted with either a plastic dough blade or a standard metal chopping blade. Hand kneading or using a stand mixer with a dough hook will not yield a sufficient level of gluten development in these recipes.

Meat Analogue Cooking Methods
Simmering, Baking, Steaming, and Combination Methods

Wheat gluten is not digestible in its raw state; therefore, it must be cooked. For seitan, the traditional method is simmering the dough in a seasoned broth. A very gentle simmer is essential when cooking seitan using this method alone.

This means that the cooking pot needs to be monitored closely and the heat regulated to maintain the gentle simmer.

Rapid simmering or boiling will produce a spongy texture and no amount of panfrying will save the finished product. On the other hand, merely poaching seitan in hot broth without simmering will produce a tough, rubbery texture, as not enough liquid will be absorbed.

Through a great deal of experimentation with cooking techniques using gluten and blends of gluten and tofu, I discovered that improved meat-like textures could be produced using a combination cooking method that includes both baking and simmering. With this combination method, baking the dough seals in the ingredients and sets the texture, while simmering completes the cooking process and maintains an ideal moisture content.

Baking also regulates the amount of liquid the dough will absorb, creating dense, meaty textures while preventing spongy finished textures. While a gentle (but active) simmer is still recommended, the temperature of the simmering broth is not as critical since baking has already set the texture of the dough. However, merely poaching in hot broth should be avoided, since not enough liquid will be absorbed to yield the best finished texture. Please note that the combination cooking method is not required for all recipes.

Meat analogues containing gluten will expand up to twice their size through absorption of the broth during simmering. The broth recipes offered are generously seasoned to enhance the flavor of the finished meat analogue. Broths with little flavor will leach the seasonings from the dough.

Simmering broths made from scratch are recommended since the complex flavor of the broth is infused into the meat analogue as it simmers. Nothing quite compares to the comforting aroma of a homemade broth filling the kitchen. The recipes for the simmering broths can be found with the recipes for each specific meat analogue being prepared. They're easy to make, but they do involve some chopping of vegetables and about an hour of cooking time. I realize that busy schedules and time constraints don't always allow the home cook to prepare every component of a recipe from scratch, so quick options are also provided for preparing the simmering broths.

In a hurry? If you don't have the time to prepare a simmering broth for the meat analogues, simply add 4 teaspoons sea salt or kosher salt to 12 cups of water and simmer as directed. Discard the water after simmering. You'll sacrifice some of the flavor in the process, so be sure to marinate or season the meat analogue when finishing it.

An important factor is the quality of water used for preparing meat analogues and simmering broths (or any recipe, for that matter). Avoid unfiltered tap water if at all possible, since tap water can be full of impurities. Faucet-mounted filters are a godsend for ensuring clean water. They're also economical and kinder to the environment than disposable plastic water containers.

Oven baking is used for some meat analogues (pressure cooking may be recommended as the best choice or offered as an alternative, depending on the recipe). In many recipes, the dough is wrapped in aluminum foil before being placed in the oven (or pressure cooker or conventional steamer). This not only creates and holds the shape of the analogue, but it also seals in moisture.

It's very important to use heavy-duty aluminum foil when you are oven baking meat analogues. Standard foil may be weak and flimsy and can easily rupture from expansion of the dough as it cooks (especially with gluten-and-tofu blends) and from the steam pressure that builds up inside the foil. Always err on using too much foil rather than not enough, and, when in doubt, wrap with an additional sheet of foil. Pressure cooking can be a bit more forgiving since the pressure inside the cooker prevents the foil from rupturing as easily; but the dough will still expand, so sturdy foil is recommended.

Meat analogue recipes that require oven baking or offer it as an option have been tested in my own home oven, which is calibrated to the correct temperature with the convection fan turned off. Convection or fan-assisted ovens are more efficient at distributing heat evenly around food by circulating hot air with a fan, which removes the blanket of cooler air surrounding food when it's first placed in the oven. This allows food to cook more evenly at a lower temperature than in a conventional oven (this is known as convective heat transfer). For this reason, baking meat analogues in a convection oven at the same temperature as a radiant-heat oven can lead to overcooking and dry results. To avoid overcooking, switch the fan off or lower the oven temperature 25 degrees F (10 degrees C) or more, depending on the desired results.

Conventional steam cooking is used for preparing the individual hand-rolled sausages. You will need a large pot with a lid and a steamer insert for this method. The seasoned dough is either wrapped or rolled in aluminum foil before being steamed. The sausages can also be steamed in a pressure cooker.

Standard or heavy-duty aluminum foil can be used for wrapping the sausages before steaming, but pop-up aluminum foil is more convenient and easier to manage. Pop-up foil is commonly used in the restaurant industry for wrapping baked potatoes. It's very convenient because cutting foil to create wrappers is not required.

Although pop-up foil is not available in all supermarkets, it is commonly used in hair salons for coloring hair and can be found in beauty supply stores or purchased online. Pop-up foil is very thin and flimsy, so double-wrapping the sausages is required so they do not burst open while steaming.

Some people may be concerned about their food coming into contact with aluminum foil. If this is a personal concern or you have any doubt, there is a simple solution: cut a piece of parchment paper to line the foil before rolling or wrapping. This will keep the dough from coming into contact with the aluminum foil. However, the foil is still required for the outer layer.

Some meat analogues will need to be refrigerated for 8 hours after the basic preparation and before finishing, so plan accordingly. Refrigeration firms the structure of the cooked gluten, thereby optimizing its texture. Don't rush or omit this step when it's recommended.

Most prepared meat analogues benefit from finishing in some manner before serving. This can include pan-glazing, sautéing, frying, broiling, pan grilling, or outdoor grilling. Always use a nonstick skillet or grill pan or a well-seasoned cast-iron skillet, since meat analogues are notorious for sticking to stainless steel (even with cooking oil).

For outdoor grilling, brush or rub the grill grates with cooking oil. Brush meat analogues with cooking oil before broiling or outdoor grilling. This applies even if the meat analogue was marinated or a sauce is being used. There is very little fat content in meat analogues, other than the trivial amount of oil that is added during preparation, and plant fat (oil) is what will keep the "meat" tender, juicy, and flavorful.

Pressure Cooking Meat Analogues

Pressure cookers work on one basic principle: steam pressure. A sealed pot, heated by an electrical heating element or on the stovetop, generates steam under pressure, which helps food cook faster. The sealed pot is constructed with a safety valve that controls the steam pressure inside.

Pressure cooking can be used to quickly simulate the effects of long braising (which refers to oven cooking foods partially submerged in liquid). Almost any food that can be cooked in steam or water-based liquids can be cooked in a pressure cooker. Foil-wrapped meat analogues that are typically baked or steamed can also be cooked in a pressure cooker, but different rules apply.

Electric programmable pressure cookers (for example, the Instant Pot) automatically regulate the internal steam pressure and are essentially a "set it and forget it" cooking method. If you wish to use a stove-top pressure cooker, please refer to the operating manual that came with it.

All of the foil-wrapped meat analogues in this cookbook are cooked on the "high" pressure setting, and you will need to set the timer on the cooker manually. If the cooker has preset cooking options, choose the "chicken" option and manually override the timer setting according to the recipe.

The high-pressure steam of pressure cooking has two major effects:

1. It increases the boiling point of the water or other liquid in the pot from 212 degrees F (100 degrees C) to 250 degrees F (121 degrees C). Exposed foods are subjected to this higher boiling temperature, and this causes the food to cook faster.

2. This increased steam pressure forces liquid into foods that are exposed to the steam. This not only helps the food cook faster but it also tenderizes certain foods such as grains, legumes, and vegetables much faster than by conventional steaming or simmering.

However, meat analogues sealed in foil packages respond differently than exposed foods. In a sealed package, the gluten dough (or gluten-and-tofu combination) is not directly exposed to the steam because the foil serves as a moisture barrier. The water in the pressure cooker is not being forced into the dough. Therefore, the package is simply being steamed at a pressurized boiling temperature of 250 degrees F (120 degrees C), as opposed to being steamed in a conventional steamer at 212 degrees F (100 degrees C) or baked in an oven at a temperature of 350 degrees F (175 degrees C), which fluctuates up and down during baking.

While pressure cooking may cook the dough faster than a conventional steamer, it will not necessarily cook the dough faster than an oven set at 350 degrees F (175 degrees C). Therefore, foil-wrapped dough still requires pressure cooking for the suggested cooking time in order for it to properly cook all the way through. While it may seem unusual to pressure cook foods for an hour and a half, for example, it is important to remember that you're not cooking exposed foods—you're cooking gluten dough sealed in a foil package.

Pressure Cooking versus Oven Baking

Pressure cooking foil-wrapped meat analogues has several advantages compared to oven baking. Foremost is that with pressure cooking the packages of foil-wrapped meat analogues have less likelihood of bursting. Improperly or insufficiently wrapped meat analogues can cause steam pressure to build up inside of the package. When the pressure inside the package is greater than the surrounding pressure of the oven, the package may burst. This not only ruins the finished product but can create a big mess in the oven. With pressure cooking, the pressure inside the cooking chamber is greater than that within the foil package, so bursting is less likely. (However, rupturing of the foil can still occur if the package is wrapped improperly or insufficiently.)

Pressure cooking provides more uniform and consistent heat. Some ovens have inconsistent temperatures or run too hot, which could cause the final product to be dry and bready rather than moist and meaty. If your oven runs too hot, decrease the oven temperature by 25 degrees F (10 degrees C). If that doesn't resolve the issue, pressure cooking may be your best option.

Another distinct advantage of pressure cooking is that it doesn't heat up the kitchen the way an oven does. That is especially appreciated during the warm months of summer.

I don't recommend using parchment paper as the only wrapping barrier inside the cooking chamber; use it only as a barrier between the dough and foil. The recipes contain a precise amount of water, and because parchment paper can get soggy, it could allow excess moisture to be forced into the dough during pressure cooking.

Shelf Life of Meat Analogues

"Shelf life" refers to the length of time that a food may be stored without becoming unfit for consumption. However, shelf life alone is not an accurate indicator of how long a food can safely be stored. Many foods can remain fresh for several days past their recommended shelf life if they are stored and refrigerated properly. However, if foods have already been contaminated with harmful bacteria, the guideline becomes irrelevant.

Meat analogues should be cooled in their simmering broth or sealed foil packages until lukewarm before being refrigerated. Simmering broths should also be cooled to lukewarm before being refrigerated. The refrigerated shelf life for gluten-and-soy-based analogues is one week; for gluten-based analogues it is ten days.

Pressure Cooking versus Simmering

In my humble opinion, the joy of cooking not only involves eating and enjoying the food we create but also experiencing the cooking process and being actively involved in it. There are some methods that I don't feel can be improved upon, and this is one of them. If we're always looking to change the process for the sake of convenience and time management, or simply because it's the latest trend, we lose a great deal from the experience. For example, there's nothing quite like the aroma of a fragrant broth filling the kitchen while it's simmering in the pot.

Visually managing the cooking process is important, too, because you can see what's going on in the pot, but with a sealed cooking chamber (as with a pressure cooker), you can't. When meat analogues are simmered, the broth is gradually absorbed by the dough in a controlled manner, whereas in a sealed pressure cooker, the broth is forced into the dough under pressure.

Many electric pressure cookers offer an option for open cooking with a "simmer" setting, and that may work, although it could be more difficult to quickly adjust the simmering temperature as needed. For the sake of convenience, or for "set it and forget it" cooking, a slow cooker (or a pressure cooker with a slow cooker option) may be a better choice since it will cook slowly and gently.

As a chef, I'm a bit "old school" when it comes to tried-and-true methods. Don't get me wrong—the pressure cooker is excellent for specific cooking applications, just not all applications. If you choose to experiment with this method as an alternative to simmering, that is entirely up to you, and I wish you much success.

All meat analogues can be frozen for up to three months and then thawed in the refrigerator and reheated or finished at your convenience. Simmering broths can be frozen for up to three months.

Preparing Tofu for Meat Analogue Recipes

Extra-firm, water-packed block tofu is used in many of the meat analogue recipes in this cookbook and can be found in the refrigerated section of the market. Do not confuse this with extra-firm silken tofu, which is a delicate, custard-like Japanese tofu. Silken tofu will not work as an alternative to the extra-firm block tofu called for in the recipes.

Before using it in the recipes, the extra-firm block tofu will need to be pressed to remove as much water as possible. It may seem redundant to press the water from the tofu only to add water back when preparing the recipes. However, the reason for this is very simple: Removing the soaking water removes any excess coagulant used in making the tofu. Also, water content in tofu varies from brand to brand and even from block to block. By removing the liquid from the tofu, weighing it, and then adding back a precise amount of water, the recipe's results remain consistent.

When weighing tofu for the recipes, minor weight variations are acceptable and will not negatively affect the recipe results. Be sure to weigh the tofu after pressing it, unless otherwise indicated. A precision digital ounce and gram scale is recommended for accuracy.

Pressing can be done ahead of time using a tofu press (allow a few hours of pressing time). Alternatively, the tofu can be wrapped in several layers of paper towels or a lint-free kitchen towel and pressed on a flat surface using the palms of your hands, assisted by your upper body weight. The advantage of using a tofu press first is that it will remove a substantial amount water, which then saves on paper towel usage.

Since the tofu press will only remove the excess water, the tofu may still contain too much moisture for the recipes. This needs to be removed by wrapping the tofu in a few layers of paper towels or a lint-free kitchen towel and pressing it on a flat surface using the palms of your hands, assisted by your upper body weight. When pressed sufficiently, the tofu should feel barely damp and have a crumbly texture. If you press the tofu ahead of time, put it in an air-tight container and store it in the refrigerator for up to three days until you're ready to use it.

Some stores now offer commercially pre-pressed extra-firm block tofu, but this tofu is often excessively dry and can negatively affect recipe results. Pressing water-packed tofu manually at home is recommended.

Basic Chikun Dough

C hikun is a versatile, plant-based meat created from a blend of vital wheat gluten, tofu, and select seasonings. It has a realistic texture and color and a minimal wheat undertaste. The basic dough can be formed into a variety of shapes, such as cutlets, nuggets, or drumsticks. The dough is lightly and neutrally seasoned, so you can add more seasonings or marinate it before it is grilled, sautéed, fried, or stewed. The dough is shaped, partially baked to seal in the ingredients and set the texture, and then simmered in broth to complete the cooking process before it is finished or used in recipes. A blender or a food processor fitted with a plastic dough blade or with a standard chopping blade is needed for this recipe.

1 cup (150 g) **vital wheat gluten**

5 ounces (142 g) pressed extra-firm block **tofu** (see page 11)

⅔ cup (160 ml) **water**

1 tablespoon neutral **vegetable oil**

1 tablespoon **nutritional yeast flakes**

2 teaspoons **onion powder**

1¼ teaspoons **sea salt** or **kosher salt**

1 teaspoon **garlic powder**

¼ teaspoon **poultry seasoning** or **Aromatica** (page 161)

BLENDER METHOD

Put the vital wheat gluten in a large bowl. Set aside.

Crumble the tofu into a blender. Add the water, oil, nutritional yeast, onion powder, salt, garlic powder, and poultry seasoning. Process until smooth and creamy. Stop the blender as necessary to scrape down the jar.

Scoop the tofu mixture into the vital wheat gluten and combine with a sturdy silicone spatula until the tofu mixture is incorporated and a ball of dough begins to form. The mixture may seem a bit dry at first; do not add more water.

Transfer the dough to a work surface. Knead vigorously for 3 to 4 minutes. This step is very important in order to develop the gluten. Test the dough by stretching it. If it tears easily, more kneading is required. Alternatively, put the dough in the bowl of a stand mixer fitted with a dough hook and process on low speed for 1 minute. Shape the dough into cutlets, tenders, or nuggets (see page 19).

FOOD PROCESSOR METHOD

Crumble the tofu into a food processor fitted with a plastic dough blade or standard chopping blade and process into fine crumbles. Add $\frac{1}{3}$ cup of the water and the oil, nutritional yeast, onion powder, salt, garlic powder, and poultry seasoning. Process until as smooth as possible. Stop to scrape down the work bowl as needed.

Add the vital wheat gluten to the tofu mixture along with the remaining $\frac{1}{3}$ cup water. Process for 1 minute. Transfer the dough to a work surface and shape it into cutlets, tenders, or nuggets (see page 19).

Tips from Chef Skye ▪ For faster prep, replace the nutritional yeast, onion powder, salt, garlic powder, and poultry seasoning with 2 tablespoons Instant Chikun Bouillon Powder (page 183).

Chikun Simmering Broth

C hikun simmering broth is used for simmering Basic Chikun Dough (page 14) as part of the preparation process. It can also be used as a base for soups, stews, and golden-colored sauces and gravies. Alternatively, it can be used in any recipe calling for chicken broth. Additional herbs or spices can be included to accommodate specific regional cuisines.

12 cups **water**

3 large **onions**, peeled and chopped

3 ribs **celery**, chopped

1 large **carrot**, unpeeled and chopped

¼ cup **nutritional yeast flakes**

6 cloves **garlic**, crushed

4 teaspoons **sea salt** or **kosher salt**, plus more as needed

1 tablespoon **organic sugar**

1 teaspoon whole **black peppercorns**

1 teaspoon **dried rubbed sage**

3 sprigs **fresh thyme**, or ½ teaspoon **dried thyme**

1 small sprig **fresh rosemary**

Small handful **parsley stems**

Put all the ingredients in a large pot, cover, and simmer over medium-low heat for 1 hour. Season with additional salt to taste. Remove the larger solids with a slotted spoon before adding the chikun.

After simmering the chikun, let the broth cool, then strain it into a sealable container to remove any remaining solids, and refrigerate. During this time, any sediment from the seasonings will settle on the bottom of the container.

The broth can be refrigerated for 1 week or frozen for up to 3 months. To use, decant the clear portion and discard the fine sediment. Be sure to add back water as necessary before using, since the broth will have become concentrated from evaporation during simmering.

If you're using the broth immediately for other purposes, such as soups or stews, strain it through a fine sieve into a clean pot and discard the solids.

Tips from Chef Skye
- Replace the sage, thyme, and rosemary with ¾ teaspoon poultry seasoning or Aromatica (page 161) if desired.

QUICK BROTH ALTERNATIVES: Homemade broth is always best and recommended. However, for the sake of convenience and expediency, a quick chikun simmering broth can be made with commercial no-chicken bouillon paste (1 teaspoon to 1 cup water) or no-chicken broth cubes (½ cube to 1 cup water).

VARIATION: For instant, homemade chikun broth, try Instant Chikun Bouillon Powder (page 183). Add additional herbs and spices as desired to accommodate specific regional cuisines, and season the prepared broth with salt to taste.

Chikun Cutlets, Tenders, or Nuggets

F or this application, Basic Chikun Dough is cut and shaped, partially baked, and then simmered in broth to complete the cooking process prior to finishing or using in recipes. Sorry, pressure cooking is not an alternative to baking the dough; an oven is required. *NOTE: Chikun Cutlets, Tenders, or Nuggets must be refrigerated for 8 hours prior to finishing to optimize their texture, so plan accordingly.*

Basic Chikun Dough (page 14)
12 cups **Chikun Simmering Broth** (page 16)

Put a stainless-steel cooling rack on a baking sheet and line the rack with parchment paper or a silicone baking mat. The cooling rack is not required, but it is recommended because it will prevent the excessive browning that would occur from direct contact with the hot baking sheet. Preheat the oven to 350 degrees F (175 degrees C).

Shape the dough into cutlets, tenders, or nuggets (see opposite page) and arrange them in a single layer on the parchment paper or baking mat. Loosely lay parchment paper or foil over the cutlets, tenders, or nuggets. Bake on the middle oven rack for 20 minutes and then remove from the oven. Slight puffing of the dough while it bakes is normal; excessive puffing indicates that the oven is too hot.

While the chikun is baking, bring the broth to a boil. If the broth was made from scratch, use a slotted spoon to remove the larger solids. It's not necessary to strain the broth completely until later.

The chikun will be soft at this stage, so handle it carefully. Lower the chikun pieces into the boiling broth and immediately decrease the heat to maintain a gentle simmer. Cook uncovered for 20 minutes; do not boil. Turn the pieces occasionally once they float to the top of the pot to ensure even cooking. When the chikun is done simmering, remove the pot from the heat, cover, and let the chikun cool in the broth.

Transfer the chikun to a food storage bag and refrigerate for 8 hours to optimize the texture before finishing. Add a marinade at this time if desired. Strain the cooled broth into a sealable container and refrigerate for future use. The cutlets, tenders, or nuggets are now ready to be seasoned and finished as desired.

How to Shape Chikun Dough

CUTLETS: Divide the dough into 6 equal pieces. Flatten the pieces with the palm of your hand. Stretch the dough against the work surface and form into cutlet shapes. If the dough is resistant to shaping, let it rest a few minutes to relax the gluten. Place the cutlets in a single layer on the parchment paper or baking mat.

TENDERS: Tenders are narrow strips of chikun. They're thicker than cutlets and longer than nuggets and are ideal for breading and frying. Divide the dough into 8 equal pieces. Stretch a piece of dough until it begins to tear and then let it contract. Don't try to smooth the surface, as bumps and irregularities will yield a better finished texture and appearance. Place the tender on the parchment paper or baking mat and repeat with the remaining dough, arranging the tenders in a single layer.

NUGGETS: Nuggets are one- or two-bite pieces of chikun. Divide the dough into 4 equal pieces. Tear each piece into 6 nuggets (tearing the dough yields a better finished texture than slicing). Place the nuggets in a single layer on the parchment paper or baking mat.

Chikun Souvlaki

This popular Greek dish features skewered Chikun Nuggets that are marinated in a garlicky citrus, white wine, and herb blend before being grilled. Serve it with toasted pita bread, sliced onions, tomatoes, cucumbers, kalamata olives, and Greek Tzatziki Sauce (page 175).

MARINADE

¼ cup freshly squeezed **lemon juice**

¼ cup **dry white wine** (such as Chardonnay or Sauvignon Blanc)

4 cloves **garlic**

1 tablespoon **dried oregano**

1 teaspoon fresh **lemon zest**

1 teaspoon **sea salt** or **kosher salt**

½ teaspoon **ground rosemary**

½ teaspoon **paprika**

½ teaspoon coarsely ground **black pepper**

CHIKUN

24 prepared Chikun Nuggets (page 18)

Put all the marinade ingredients in a blender and process until smooth. Pour into a food storage bag and add the Chikun Nuggets. Press the air out of the bag, seal, and refrigerate for 8 to 12 hours.

Thread the nuggets on skewers and brush with olive oil. Grill or broil as desired. For outdoor grilling, spray or rub the grill grates with cooking oil or use a nonstick grill mat.

Chikun Drumsticks or Drumettes

Drumsticks and drumettes are prepared by wrapping basic chikun dough around wooden craft sticks (for drumsticks) or hors d'oeuvre sticks (for drumettes). They're partially baked and then simmered in broth to complete the cooking process before being coated with batter and fried or finished on the grill. Pressure cooking is not an option for this recipe; an oven is required. *NOTE: Drumsticks or drumettes must be refrigerated for 8 hours prior to finishing to optimize their texture, so plan accordingly.*

Basic Chikun Dough (page 14)
12 cups **Chikun Simmering Broth** (page 16)

For drumsticks, have ready six wooden craft sticks (the type used for ice-cream treats). For drumettes (mini drumsticks), have ready 12 wooden hors d'oeuvre sticks.

Put a stainless-steel cooling rack on a baking sheet. The cooling rack is not required, but it is recommended for propping up the drumsticks or drumettes to prevent flat spots caused by contact with the baking surface. It will also prevent excessive browning, which would occur from direct contact with the hot baking sheet. If you don't have a cooling rack, line the baking sheet with a silicone baking mat or with parchment paper. Preheat the oven to 350 degrees F (175 degrees C).

With a sharp knife, divide the Basic Chikun Dough into 6 equal pieces for drumsticks or 12 equal pieces for drumettes. Stretch a piece of dough as far as it can be stretched without tearing completely and then twist and wind it around a stick (if the dough tears too easily, it requires additional kneading). Be sure to leave about ½ inch of the stick free for grasping. Wind the dough narrow at the bottom and thicker toward the top to create a drumstick shape. Pinch the end of the dough so it doesn't unwind.

Insert the free end of the sticks into the slots in the rack, propping up the drumsticks or drumettes at a slight angle. Space them so they do not touch each other.

Bake uncovered on the middle oven rack for 20 minutes for drumsticks or 15 minutes for drumettes and then remove from the oven. Slight puffing of the dough as it bakes is normal; excessive puffing indicates that the oven is too hot.

Bring the broth to a boil. If the broth was made from scratch, use a slotted spoon to remove the larger solids. It's not necessary to strain the broth until later. The chikun will be soft at this stage, so handle it carefully.

Lower the pieces into the boiling broth and immediately decrease the heat to maintain a gentle simmer. Cook uncovered for 20 minutes; do not boil. Turn the pieces occasionally once they float to the top of the pot. After the pieces have simmered, remove the pot from the heat, cover, and let the chikun cool in the broth.

Transfer the drumsticks or drumettes to a food storage bag and refrigerate for 8 hours to optimize the texture before finishing. Add a marinade at this time if desired. Strain the cooled broth into a sealable container and refrigerate for future use. The drumsticks or drumettes are now ready to be seasoned and finished as desired.

Chikun Piccata

Piccata refers to a method of preparing food in a piquant sauce. For this dish, tender Chikun Cutlets are lightly breaded, pan browned, and served with a tangy sauce consisting of seasoned broth, white wine, lemon juice, nondairy butter, capers, and parsley. Try serving it over cooked pasta or rice.

4 prepared **Chikun Cutlets** (page 18)

Coarsely ground **black pepper**

1 tablespoon **all-purpose flour**, plus more for dredging

¼ cup mild **olive oil**

1 **shallot**, finely chopped, or ¼ cup finely chopped **red onion**

3 cloves **garlic**, minced

½ cup **Chikun Simmering Broth** (page 16)

6 tablespoons **dry white wine** (such as Chardonnay or Sauvignon Blanc) **or** additional broth

2 tablespoons freshly squeezed **lemon juice**

2 tablespoons **capers**, drained

2 tablespoons **nondairy butter** or **margarine**

¼ cup chopped **fresh parsley**, lightly packed

Lemon slices, for garnish

Season the cutlets with pepper. Dredge lightly in flour, shaking off any excess.

Put the oil in a large skillet and place over medium heat. When the oil is hot, add the cutlets and cook, turning every few minutes, until the chikun is lightly browned all over. Transfer to a plate and cover to keep warm.

Put the the shallot and garlic in the skillet and sauté over medium heat until the shallot is translucent. Sprinkle the 1 tablespoon flour over the shallot and garlic, stir to combine, and cook for 1 minute.

Incorporate the chikun broth in increments while stirring vigorously. Add the wine, lemon juice, and capers, and bring to a boil. Whisk in the butter until melted and simmer until the sauce thickens a bit, about 5 minutes. Stir in the parsley.

Arrange the chikun on serving plates, pour the sauce over the top, and garnish with lemon slices. Serve immediately.

Chikun Piccata

Chikun Yakitori

Y akitori is a Japanese dish consisting of marinated, skewered, and grilled nuggets of chikun garnished with chopped scallions and sesame seeds. Four bamboo skewers are needed for this recipe.

¼ cup **Chikun Simmering Broth** (page 16)

¼ cup **tamari**, **soy sauce**, or **Bragg Liquid Aminos**

¼ cup **mirin** (Japanese sweet rice wine) or **dry sherry**, or 2 tablespoons **lemon juice**

1 tablespoon **dark brown sugar**

3 cloves **garlic**

2 teaspoons grated **fresh ginger** (see page 31)

2 teaspoons **cornstarch** or **unmodified potato starch**

1 teaspoon **sambal oelek** (Indonesian chile sauce), **sriracha sauce**, or other hot sauce

24 prepared **Chikun Nuggets** (page 18)

Chopped **scallions**, for garnish

Sesame seeds, for garnish

Soak 4 bamboo skewers in water for several hours before grilling to discourage the wood from burning.

To make the marinade, put the broth, tamari, mirin, brown sugar, garlic, ginger, starch, and sambal oelek in a blender and process until smooth. Pour into a food storage bag and add the Chikun Nuggets. Press the air out of the bag, seal, and refrigerate for 2 to 12 hours before grilling or broiling.

Thread 4 Chikun Nuggets on each skewer. Reserve the marinade for the dipping sauce. To make the sauce, put the reserved marinade in a small saucepan over medium heat and bring to a simmer. Remove from the heat and set aside until serving time.

Broil or grill the skewered chikun, turning it occasionally, until golden brown. Garnish with scallions and sesame seeds and serve with the dipping sauce.

Tips from Chef Skye

- Brush the skewered chikun with oil before broiling or grilling to keep it moist.

- For pan grilling, oil a nonstick grill pan. For outdoor grilling, rub the grill grates with cooking oil or use a nonstick grill mat.

Seasoned Breaded Fried Chikun

 The breading in this recipe creates a light and crispy coating on fried chikun.

¾ cup **all-purpose flour**

1 cup plain **nondairy milk**

1½ cups very fine plain dry **bread crumbs**

2 teaspoons **onion powder**

2 teaspoons **sea salt** or **kosher salt**

1 teaspoon **garlic powder**

1 teaspoon **paprika**

1 teaspoon coarsely ground **black pepper**

Prepared **Chikun Cutlets, Tenders, or Nuggets** (page 18), or
prepared **Chikun Drumsticks or Drumettes** (page 22)

For the breading, put the flour and milk in a medium bowl and whisk to make a smooth batter. Put the bread crumbs, onion powder, salt, garlic powder, paprika, and pepper in a separate medium bowl. Dip the chikun in the batter, shake off the excess, and then dredge in the bread-crumb mixture, coating each piece evenly. Set aside on a plate to dry for 10 minutes.

Put enough cooking oil in a deep fryer, deep skillet, or wok to reach a depth of 2 inches. Place over medium-high heat until the oil is shimmering. (Test it with some bread crumbs; if they rise and begin to brown fairly quickly, the oil is sufficiently hot.) Fry the chikun in the hot oil, turning each piece occasionally, until golden brown. Transfer to a plate lined with several layers of paper towels to drain. Serve hot or cold.

Indian Butter Chikun

Tender sliced chikun is cooked in a deliciously rich and fragrant tomato-cashew cream sauce. This dish is traditionally served over basmati rice with a side of naan bread. It's an excellent introduction to Indian cuisine because the seasonings are not overwhelming to most timid palates.

½ cup (2½ ounces by weight) **raw cashews**

2 teaspoons **Garam Masala** (page 162) or commercial equivalent

1 teaspoon **ground cumin**

1 teaspoon **ground turmeric**

½ teaspoon **ground fenugreek**

⅛ teaspoon **cayenne**

1½ cups **Chikun Simmering Broth** (page 16)

1 tablespoon freshly squeezed **lemon juice**

¼ cup mild **olive oil**

4 prepared **Chikun Cutlets** (page 18), sliced

1 medium **yellow onion**, cut in half and thinly sliced

1 tablespoon grated **fresh ginger** (see page 31)

3 cloves **garlic**, minced

2 tablespoons **nondairy butter** or **margarine**

1 can (15 ounces) **tomato sauce**

Sea salt or **kosher salt**

To soften the cashews, put them in a bowl and add just enough water to cover them. Let soak in the refrigerator for 8 hours. To expedite softening, put the cashews in a heatproof bowl, cover with boiling water, and let soak for 30 minutes.

Put the Garam Masala, cumin, turmeric, fenugreek, and cayenne in a small bowl and stir to combine. Set aside.

Drain the cashews, discarding the soaking water, and put in a blender. Add the broth and lemon juice and process for 2 minutes. Set aside.

Put 2 tablespoons of the oil in a large nonstick skillet over medium heat. Lightly brown the chikun in the oil. Remove and set aside.

Put the remaining 2 tablespoons of oil and the reserved spice mixture in the same skillet over medium heat and stir until very fragrant, about 1 minute. Add the onion and sauté until softened, about 5 minutes. Add the ginger and garlic and sauté for 1 minute. Add the butter and stir until melted.

Add the tomato sauce and stir until combined. Add the chikun, increase the heat slightly to bring the sauce to a simmer, and then decrease the heat to just above low. Cover the skillet and cook for 20 minutes, stirring occasionally.

Stir in the cashew cream mixture, increase the heat to bring to a simmer, and cook, stirring frequently, until the sauce is thickened, about 5 minutes. Season with additional cayenne and salt to taste.

How to Grate Fresh Ginger

With a paring knife, slice away the tough skin. Put a box grater over a clean work surface and grate the ginger on the second-to-smallest holes of the grater. The fibrous material will remain on the outside of the grater; dispose of the fibrous material. The ginger pulp will either fall to the work surface or collect on the inside of the grater. Using your fingers, reach inside the grater and scrape out the pulp. Measure the amount needed and proceed with the recipe.

Kung Pao Chikun

 For this classic take-out dish, diced chikun, sliced garlic, fresh ginger, and green onions are stir-fried in a spicy Szechuan sauce with dry-roasted peanuts. Serve it with steamed jasmine rice.

SZECHUAN SAUCE

¼ cup **water**

1 tablespoon **dark brown sugar**

1 tablespoon **rice vinegar**

1 tablespoon **dry sherry**, **Shaoxing rice wine**, or **water**

1 tablespoon **tamari**, **soy sauce**, or **Bragg Liquid Aminos**

1 teaspoon **sesame oil**

1 teaspoon **cornstarch** or **unmodified potato starch**

STIR-FRIED CHIKUN

¼ cup **cornstarch** or **unmodified potato starch**, for dusting the chikun

12 ounces prepared **Chikun Cutlets or Tenders** (page 18), diced into ½-inch pieces

2 tablespoons **cooking oil**

1 teaspoon **sesame oil**

1 teaspoon coarsely ground **black pepper**

1 to 2 teaspoons crushed **red pepper flakes** (depending on heat preference)

5 **scallions** including green tops, chopped

1 tablespoon grated fresh **ginger** (see page 31)

4 cloves **garlic**, thinly sliced

⅓ cup unsalted **dry-roasted peanuts**

For the sauce, put all the ingredients in a small bowl and whisk thoroughly to ensure the starch is fully dissolved. Set aside.

For the chikun, put the starch in a deep bowl or food storage bag. Add the chikun (seal the bag, if using) and toss until evenly dusted.

Put the cooking oil and sesame oil in a wok or deep skillet over medium heat. When hot, add the black pepper and red pepper flakes and cook for 30 seconds. Add the chikun and stir-fry until it is lightly browned.

Add the scallions, ginger, and garlic and stir-fry for 1 to 2 minutes. Add the sauce mixture, toss well, and cook until the sauce begins to thicken. Fold in the peanuts. Serve immediately.

Thai Green Curry

Commercial Thai green curry paste is made from a blend of green chiles, Thai ginger (galangal), lemongrass, and kaffir lime; it can be found in most supermarkets. This fragrant Thai curry with chikun is superb served with steamed jasmine rice.

1 tablespoon **cooking oil**

1 medium **onion**, peeled and sliced

1 can (13 to 14 ounces) unsweetened **coconut milk**

1½ cups **Chikun Simmering Broth** (page 16)

3 tablespoons **Thai green curry paste**

1 tablespoon **coconut palm sugar** or **light brown sugar**

1 medium **zucchini**, halved lengthwise and sliced

½ cup fresh or thawed frozen **green peas**

¼ teaspoon crushed **red pepper flakes** (use more if you like additional heat)

4 prepared **Chikun Cutlets** (page 18), sliced

3 tablespoons freshly squeezed **lime juice**

Sea salt or **kosher salt**

¼ cup chopped fresh **Thai basil** or **sweet basil**, for garnish

¼ cup chopped **fresh cilantro**, for garnish

Put the oil in a large pot over medium-low heat. Add the onion and let it sweat (low sizzle; no browning) until tender, about 10 minutes.

Add the coconut milk, broth, curry paste, sugar, zucchini, peas, and red pepper flakes. Bring to a gentle simmer, partially cover, and cook for 15 minutes.

Add the chikun and lime juice. Return to a simmer and cook uncovered for 15 minutes. Season with salt to taste. Ladle into bowls and garnish with the basil and cilantro.

Tandoori Chikun

YIELDS 3 TO 6 SERVINGS

Tandoori is a dish originating from the Indian subcontinent. The name comes from *tandoor*, the cylindrical clay oven in which the dish is traditionally prepared. Here, the chikun is pan grilled rather than oven baked and is garnished with cilantro, onion, and lemon wedges. The marinade consists of a quick, tangy "yogurt" made by curdling soymilk with apple cider vinegar and is seasoned with a blend of spices called *tandoori masala*. Beet powder is included for color.

MARINADE

¾ cup plain **nondairy milk** (soymilk is recommended)

¼ cup **apple cider vinegar**

1 tablespoon **smoked paprika**

1 tablespoon **beet powder** (optional)

1 teaspoon **sea salt** or **kosher salt**

1 teaspoon **onion powder**

1 teaspoon **ground turmeric**

1 teaspoon **ground ginger**

1 teaspoon **ground coriander**

1 teaspoon **ground cumin**

½ teaspoon **garlic powder**

¼ teaspoon **cayenne**

CHIKUN AND GARNISHES

Prepared **Chikun Drumsticks** or **Drumettes** (page 22)

2 tablespoons **peanut oil** or other cooking oil

Chopped **fresh cilantro**, for garnish

Sliced **white or yellow onion**, raw or lightly grilled, for garnish

Lemon wedges, for garnish

Put all the marinade ingredients in a small bowl and whisk until thickened. Transfer to a food storage bag and add the chikun. Press to remove excess air from the bag and seal. Let the chikun marinate in the refrigerator for 2 to 12 hours.

To pan grill the marinated chikun, season the grill pan with the oil and put it over medium-high heat. Grill the chikun, turning occasionally, until evenly browned all over.

Transfer the chikun to a serving platter. Garnish with cilantro, raw or lightly grilled onion, and lemon wedges.

Ethiopian Chikun

Ethiopian Chikun

 hikun Drumsticks or Drumettes (mini drumsticks) are rubbed with a traditional Ethiopian spice blend called berbere, blackened in a hot skillet, and served with wedges of fresh lemon.

3 tablespoons **Berbere Spice Blend** (page 162) or commercial equivalent

Prepared **Chikun Drumsticks or Drumettes** (page 22)

Freshly squeezed **lemon juice**

Lemon wedges, for serving

Put the berbere in a large bowl. Add the drumsticks and toss until evenly coated.

Coat the bottom of a large nonstick skillet or wok with peanut oil or other high-heat cooking oil and put over medium-high heat. When the oil is hot but not smoking, brown the drumsticks in the skillet. Transfer to a serving platter and drizzle with lemon juice. Serve with lemon wedges.

Korean Buffalo-Style Chikun Drumettes

A classic American appetizer is given an Asian twist. Lightly breaded and fried Chikun Drumettes are tossed with a spicy Korean-inspired sauce made with *gochujang* (Korean chile paste) and served with Buttermilk Ranch Dressing and crunchy crudités.

CHIKUN

Prepared **Chikun Drumettes** (page 22)

BATTER

¾ cup **unmodified potato starch** or **cornstarch**

¼ cup **white rice flour** or **all-purpose flour**

2 teaspoons **baking powder**

1½ teaspoons **sea salt** or **kosher salt**

1 teaspoon **paprika**

1 teaspoon **garlic powder**

¾ cup **water**

SAUCE

½ cup **nondairy butter** or **margarine**, melted

¼ cup **gochujang** (Korean red chile paste)

¼ cup **ketchup**

1 teaspoon **onion powder**

½ teaspoon **garlic powder**

GARNISHES AND SIDES

Chopped **scallions**

Chopped **fresh cilantro**

Buttermilk Ranch Dressing (page 190; optional)

Celery and **carrot sticks** (optional)

Put the drumettes in a food storage bag or container with a lid.

Put all the batter ingredients in a medium bowl or large measuring cup and whisk to combine. The batter will be somewhat thin. Add the batter to the bag with the drumettes, seal, and shake to evenly coat. Transfer the drumettes to a plate, shaking off any excess batter. Set aside.

Put all the sauce ingredients in a small bowl and whisk until smooth. Set aside until ready to use.

Put 2 inches of cooking oil in a deep skillet or wok over medium-high heat until shimmering. Carefully lower the drumettes into the hot oil (don't overcrowd; fry in batches) and fry until golden brown, turning occasionally with tongs or a Chinese spider (a stainless-steel ladle with an open weave).

If the oil is sufficiently hot, the batter will brown quickly, so do not leave it unattended (remember, you're only browning the batter since the chikun is already cooked). Transfer to a plate lined with paper towels to drain and let cool for a few minutes.

Toss the drummettes in the sauce just before serving. Garnish with scallions and cilantro. Serve with Buttermilk Ranch Dressing and celery and carrot sticks on the side.

Whole Roast Chikun

Whole roast chikun is created from a blend of vital wheat gluten, tofu, and select seasonings. The roast is partially baked and then simmered in broth to complete the preparation. It is finished by being wrapped in rice paper to create a "skin," pan-glazed until golden brown and crispy, and reheated in the oven before it is sliced and served. A food processor fitted with a plastic dough blade or standard chopping blade is recommended for this recipe. *NOTE: The prepared Roast Chikun must be refrigerated for 8 hours prior to finishing to optimize its texture, so plan accordingly.*

1½ cups (225 g) **vital wheat gluten**

10 ounces (284 g) extra-firm block **tofu**, pressed (see page 11)

1 cup (240 ml) **water**

2 tablespoons neutral **vegetable oil**

4 teaspoons **nutritional yeast flakes**

4 teaspoons **onion powder**

1½ teaspoons **garlic powder**

1½ teaspoons **sea salt** or **kosher salt**

½ teaspoon **poultry seasoning** or **Aromatica** (page 161)

12 cups **Chikun Simmering Broth** (page 16)

2 sheets **rice paper** (spring roll wrappers) or fresh **yuba** (tofu skin)

2 tablespoons **nondairy butter** or **margarine**

1 tablespoon **tamari**, **soy sauce**, or **Bragg Liquid Aminos**

2 tablespoons **dry white wine**, **lemon juice**, or **Chikun Simmering Broth** (page 16)

1 tablespoon minced **fresh herbs**, such as rosemary, thyme, or tarragon (optional)

Coarsely ground **black pepper** or other dry spice seasonings of choice

Put the vital wheat gluten in a large bowl. Set aside.

Crumble the tofu into a blender. Add the water, oil, nutritional yeast, onion powder, garlic powder, salt, and poultry seasoning and process until smooth and creamy. Stop the blender as necessary to scrape down the jar.

Scoop the tofu mixture into the vital wheat gluten. Combine with a sturdy silicone spatula until the tofu mixture is incorporated and a ball of dough begins to form. The mixture may seem a bit dry at first; do not add more water.

Transfer the dough to a work surface and knead vigorously for 3 to 4 minutes. This is important in order to develop the gluten. Test the dough by stretching it. If it tears easily, more kneading is required. Alternatively, put the dough into a stand mixer fitted with a dough hook and process on low speed for 1 minute.

Preheat the oven to 350 degrees F (175 degrees C).

Lay an 18-inch-long sheet of aluminum foil on a work surface (if you prefer, use 2 large sheets of parchment paper). Transfer the dough to the foil and shape into a compact oval. Roll the dough in the foil and then fold the ends under to create a package. Do not seal the package. The foil (or parchment) is being used only to hold the shape of the roast, not wrap it airtight. Put the package on a baking sheet and bake on the middle oven rack for 1 hour.

Unwrap and pierce the roast four times on the top and four times on the bottom with a fork. The roast will be very soft at this stage, so handle carefully.

Bring the broth to a boil. If the broth was made from scratch, use a slotted spoon to remove the larger solids. It's not necessary to strain the broth until later. Carefully lower the roast into the broth. Decrease the heat to maintain a simmer and cook for 1 hour. Turn the roast occasionally as it simmers.

Monitor the pot frequently and adjust the heat as necessary to maintain a simmer. The broth should be gently bubbling. Do not boil, but do not let the roast merely poach in the hot broth either, as a gentle simmer is necessary to penetrate the roast and finish the cooking process.

Remove the pot from the heat, cover, and let the roast cool in the broth. Transfer the roast to a food storage bag, seal, and refrigerate for 8 hours to optimize the texture. Strain the cooled broth into a sealable container and refrigerate for future use.

To finish the roast, bring it to room temperature for 1 hour before finishing. Preheat the oven to 350 degrees F (175 degrees C).

Put the roast on a work surface. Soak the rice paper briefly in warm water to soften. Drape over the roast, forming it over the top and tucking the ends under the bottom. The rice paper will continue to soften and become more flexible within a few minutes. The goal is to completely seal the roast with the rice paper. Stretch the softened, elastic paper as needed to achieve this goal. Alternatively, the roast can be wrapped in yuba in a similar manner. (Note that yuba does not need to be soaked.)

Put the butter in a large, deep nonstick skillet or wok over medium heat until melted. Add the roast and cook, turning occasionally, until golden all over.

Add the tamari and continue to cook and turn the roast for about 1 minute. Add the wine, optional herbs, and a few pinches of black pepper. Continue to pan-glaze until the liquid has evaporated and the roast has a beautiful golden-brown color. Be sure to run a stove exhaust fan while pan-glazing, as some smoke will be produced.

Transfer to a shallow baking dish, cover with foil, and bake for 30 minutes to heat through.

Transfer the roast to a serving platter, slice, and serve immediately.

Tips from Chef Skye
- For faster prep, replace the nutritional yeast, onion powder, garlic powder, salt, and poultry seasoning with 3 tablespoons Instant Chikun Bouillon Powder (page 183).
- Spooning hot broth over the sliced roast will keep the slices moist on the serving platter.
- Thinly sliced, cold leftover roast makes superb hot or cold sandwiches. For hot sandwiches, slice the cold roast and then wrap the slices securely in foil. Put the foil package in a hot oven or in a steamer until the slices are heated through.

Quick Dough Preparation for a Large-Capacity Food Processor

If you have a large-capacity food processor (14 cups), the dough can be mixed entirely in the food processor (no blender required). Crumble the tofu into the food processor fitted with a plastic dough blade or standard chopping blade and process into fine crumbles. Add half of the water and the oil and seasonings. Process until as smooth as possible. Stop to scrape down the work bowl as needed. Add the vital wheat gluten to the tofu mixture along with the remaining water. Process for 2 minutes. Transfer the dough to a work surface to knead and proceed with the recipe as instructed.

Shredded Chikun

S hredded chikun is one of my most popular signature recipes. The chikun, when pulled into shreds, amazingly resembles baked, shredded chicken in flavor, aroma, and texture. Shredded chikun is ideal for use in recipes for which a shredded texture is desired, such as chilled chikun salad, hot or cold wraps or sandwiches, stir-fries, flash sautés, and Mexican cuisine. The chikun can also be torn into meaty tenders or nuggets, coated with batter, and fried. A pressure cooker is recommended for preparation, although oven baking is an option. A food processor is required for this recipe to achieve the proper finished texture. If you have a large-capacity food processor, see page 42.

1½ cups (225 g) **vital wheat gluten**

10 ounces (284 g) extra-firm **tofu**, pressed (see page 11)

1¼ cups (300 ml) **water**

2 tablespoons neutral **vegetable oil**

4 teaspoons **nutritional yeast flakes**

4 teaspoons **onion powder**

1½ teaspoons **garlic powder**

1½ teaspoons **sea salt** or **kosher salt**

½ teaspoon **poultry seasoning** or **Aromatica** (page 161)

Put the vital wheat gluten in a large bowl and set aside.

Crumble the tofu into a blender. Add the water, oil, nutritional yeast, onion powder, garlic powder, salt, and poultry seasoning and process until smooth and creamy. Stop the blender as necessary to scrape down the jar.

Scoop the tofu mixture into the vital wheat gluten. Combine with a sturdy silicone spatula until the tofu mixture is incorporated and a sticky ball of dough begins to form. Let the dough rest for 5 minutes. This will give the gluten a chance to absorb the liquid and help reduce the stickiness.

Put the dough in a food processor fitted with a standard chopping blade or plastic dough blade and process for 2 minutes. If you have a small-capacity food processor, divide the dough in half and process each half separately to reduce wear and tear on the motor.

The processor may bounce as the dough reaches its desired elasticity. If it does, simply hold the processor in place. If the blade stops turning, turn the unit off; the dough should be sufficiently processed.

When the dough is sufficiently processed, it will be sticky, stretchy, glossy, and slightly warm. Occasionally, the sticky dough may creep up onto the motor shaft of the processor during processing. Simply clean it up with a damp paper towel.

To wrap the dough, lay an 18-inch-long sheet of heavy-duty aluminum foil on a work surface. Transfer the dough to the foil and shape into a compact mass. Roll the dough in the foil and twist the ends tightly to seal. Bend the twisted ends in half to lock them tight. Wrap the package in a second sheet of foil in a similar manner.

If you will be oven baking the dough (rather than pressure cooking it), twist the ends of the foil tightly but leave a small amount of air space in the package on each side to allow for expansion of the dough during baking. Wrap it in a third sheet of foil for reinforcement.

To pressure cook, put 3 cups of water in the cooker and put the trivet in place. Put the package on the trivet, seal the lid, close the steam valve, and cook on high for 90 minutes. Turn the unit off and let the pressure release naturally for 30 minutes. Remove the package and let cool until it can be handled comfortably.

To oven bake (instead of pressure cook), preheat the oven to 350 degrees F (175 degrees C). Put the foil package directly on the middle oven rack and bake for 2 hours. Remove from the oven and let cool until the package can be handled comfortably.

To shred the chikun, bend the warm roast in half and split it lengthwise to reveal the "grain." Tear the roast in half following the split. Bend and tear those pieces in half lengthwise. Pull the chikun into long strings or shreds, following the grain as much as possible. Tear those pieces into smaller bite-sized shreds, once again following the grain as much as possible. Use in recipes as desired. Store in an airtight container in the refrigerator and use within 1 week.

Tips from Chef Skye

- For faster prep, replace the nutritional yeast, onion powder, garlic powder, salt, and poultry seasoning with 3 tablespoons Instant Chikun Bouillon Powder (page 183).

- For additional flavor, use a dry seasoning rub prior to wrapping and cooking the chikun.

- For soups and stews, add Shredded Chikun just before serving to retain its texture.

Troubleshooting Tips from Chef Skye

If the finished product has a bread-like texture, it may indicate poor-quality gluten that contains too much starch. The gluten must be guaranteed a minimum of 75 percent protein. If the gluten quality is not in question, try changing the brand of tofu.

A bread-like texture could also indicate that the dough was not processed sufficiently to develop the gluten strands. A high-quality food processor is required for sufficient gluten development.

Check the oven temperature. If the oven is running too hot, adjust the temperature as needed. When baking, be sure to triple-wrap the dough with the foil and seal securely to prevent moisture loss. If you consistently have problems with oven baking, try using the pressure cooker method instead.

Tex-Mex Shredded Chikun

Tender shreds of vegan chikun are tossed with zesty seasonings for use in Tex-Mex and south-of-the-border recipes.

2 teaspoons **mild chile powder** (such as ancho)

1 teaspoon **ground cumin**

¼ teaspoon **chipotle chile powder**, or more for extra heat

2 tablespoons **cooking oil**

1 medium **onion**, halved and thinly sliced

3 cloves **garlic**, minced

12 ounces prepared **Shredded Chikun** (page 44), pulled into bite-sized shreds

2 tablespoons **water**

Sea salt or **kosher salt**

Put the mild chile powder, cumin, and chipotle chile powder in a small dish and stir to combine. Set aside.

Put the oil in a large nonstick skillet or wok over medium heat. When hot, add the onion and sauté until tender and translucent. Add the garlic and sauté for 30 seconds. Add the chikun and water. Sprinkle in the reserved chile powder blend and toss until evenly distributed.

Cook, tossing frequently, until the chikun is heated through. Season with salt to taste.

Barbecue or Teriyaki Shredded Chikun

Tender shreds of vegan chikun are tossed with tangy barbecue or teriyaki sauce. This makes an unbeatable sandwich filling and is equally wonderful served over fragrant jasmine rice.

2 tablespoons **cooking oil**

1 medium **onion**, halved and thinly sliced

3 cloves **garlic**, minced (1 tablespoon)

12 ounces prepared **Shredded Chikun** (page 44), pulled into bite-sized shreds

½ cup **barbecue sauce** or **teriyaki sauce**, plus more as desired

Put the oil in a large nonstick skillet or wok over medium heat. Add the onion and sauté until tender and translucent. Add the garlic and sauté for 30 seconds. Add the chikun and sauce and toss until evenly distributed. Cook until heated through.

Chikun and Vegetable Stir-Fry

lash-cooked vegetables and tender morsels of chikun are tossed together with an Asian-inspired sauce. Serve this stir-fry over steamed jasmine rice or cooked Asian noodles.

2 tablespoons **tamari**, **soy sauce**, or **Bragg Liquid Aminos**

1 tablespoon **mirin** (Japanese sweet rice wine)

2 tablespoons **peanut oil** or other high-heat cooking oil

2 teaspoons **sesame oil**

6 cups **stir-fry vegetables** (choose your favorites), chopped, julienned, or shredded

1 tablespoon grated **fresh ginger** (see page 31)

3 cloves **garlic**, minced

12 ounces prepared **Shredded Chikun** (page 44), torn into bite-sized pieces

1 tablespoon **sriracha sauce**, **sambal oelek**, or other **Asian red chile sauce**

Put the tamari and mirin in a small bowl and set aside. Put the peanut oil and sesame oil in a small dish and set aside.

Separate the cruciferous or crunchy vegetables from the quick-cooking tender vegetables (such as pea pods and bean sprouts) and put them into two separate bowls.

Heat a wok over medium-high heat until very hot. Put the oil mixture in the wok and swirl it around the sides of the pan. Add any cruciferous or crunchy vegetables and stir-fry until the colors are bright. Add the ginger and garlic and stir-fry for 30 seconds.

Add the chikun and the reserved tamari mixture and swirl it around the sides of the wok. Continue to stir-fry, tossing frequently, until the cruciferous vegetables are tender-crisp.

Add the quick-cooking vegetables and toss for 30 seconds. Add the sriracha sauce and toss well until evenly distributed. Remove from the heat and serve immediately.

Triple-Dip Battered Chikun

his batter recipe creates an extra-crispy seasoned coating for fried chikun. For a superb texture, try using a fifty-fifty blend of all-purpose flour and white rice flour for the dry mixture and batter.

DRY COATING

1½ cups **all-purpose flour** or **white rice flour**
(or ¾ cup each)

2 teaspoons **onion powder**

2 teaspoons **garlic powder**

2 teaspoons **sea salt** or **kosher salt**

2 teaspoons **paprika** or smoked paprika
(for a smoky flavor)

1 teaspoon coarsely ground **black pepper**

BATTER

1 cup **all-purpose flour** or **white rice flour**
(or ½ cup each)

2 teaspoons **baking powder**

1 teaspoon **sea salt** or **kosher salt**

1½ cups plain **nondairy milk** or **Quick Buttermilk**
(page 189)

CHIKUN

1½ pounds prepared **Shredded Chikun** (page 44), torn into medium-sized chunks

Put all the dry coating ingredients in a large bowl and whisk to combine.

Put all the batter ingredients in a separate large bowl and whisk until smooth (small lumps are okay). The batter will thicken while standing. A thick batter is ideal for this breading, so do not dilute with additional milk.

Dredge the chikun pieces in the dry mixture. Dip each piece into the batter until evenly coated; shake off any excess. Dredge again in the dry mixture until evenly coated and set aside on a plate. Repeat with the remaining chikun pieces.

Put 2 inches of cooking oil in a deep fryer, deep skillet, or wok over medium-high heat until shimmering (test with some bread crumbs; if they rise and begin to brown fairly quickly, the oil is sufficiently hot). Fry in the hot oil until golden brown, turning occasionally. Transfer to a plate lined with several layers of paper towels to drain. Serve hot or cold.

Mediterranean Chikun

Tender morsels of chikun are sautéed in white wine, lemon juice, and Mediterranean seasonings and then garnished with kalamata olives and parsley for a light and refreshing flavor. Serve them over orzo, couscous, or rice, and garnish with parsley and kalamata olives. The seasoned chikun can also be served hot or cold in a flatbread wrap or pita pocket with fresh or grilled vegetables and Greek Tzatziki Sauce (page 175).

2 tablespoons **dry white wine** (such as Chardonnay or Sauvignon Blanc)
or freshly squeezed **lemon juice**

1 tablespoon freshly squeezed **lemon juice**

1 teaspoon **dried basil**

1 teaspoon **dried oregano**

½ teaspoon **ground cumin**

¼ teaspoon crushed **red pepper flakes**

2 tablespoons **olive oil**

1 medium **onion**, halved and thinly sliced

3 cloves **garlic**, minced (1 tablespoon)

12 ounces prepared **Shredded Chikun** (page 44), torn into bite-sized pieces

Sea salt or **kosher salt**

Coarsely ground **black pepper**

Put the wine and lemon juice in small dish and set aside. Put the basil, oregano, cumin, and red pepper flakes in a separate small dish and set aside.

Put the oil in a large nonstick skillet or wok over medium heat. Add the onion and sauté until tender and translucent. Add the garlic and sauté for 30 seconds.

Add the chikun and sauté, tossing frequently, until lightly browned. Add the reserved wine mixture and the reserved seasonings and toss until evenly distributed. Continue to sauté until most of the liquid has evaporated but the chikun is still moist. Season with salt and pepper to taste.

Beaf

Basic Beaf Dough

Beaf is a hybrid word derived from the consonants of the word "beef" and the vowels of the word "wheat." It is a versatile, plant-based meat created from a blend of vital wheat gluten and select seasonings. The basic dough is used to create thick medallions or thin steak cutlets, steak bites (nuggets), beaf crumbles, kebabs, short ribz, and roast beaf. The dough is lightly and neutrally seasoned, so you can add more seasonings or marinate it before it is grilled, sautéed, fried, braised, or stewed, according to the specific dish being prepared. *NOTE: The prepared Basic Beaf Dough must be refrigerated for 8 hours prior to finishing to optimize its texture, so plan accordingly.* A marinade may be added at this time if desired.

DRY INGREDIENTS

1½ cups (225 g) **vital wheat gluten**

2 tablespoons **mushroom powder**

4 teaspoons **onion powder**

2 teaspoons **garlic powder**

½ teaspoon ground **white pepper**

LIQUID INGREDIENTS

1 cup (240 ml) **water**

3 tablespoons **tamari**, **soy sauce**, or **Bragg Liquid Aminos**

2 tablespoons **olive oil**

2 teaspoons **Worcestershire Sauce** (page 182) or commercial vegan equivalent

Put the dry ingredients in a large bowl and whisk to combine. Put the liquid ingredients in a small bowl or measuring cup and stir to combine.

Pour the liquid mixture into the dry ingredients and combine thoroughly with a sturdy silicone spatula to form the dough and begin developing the gluten.

Transfer the dough to a work surface and knead vigorously until very elastic. Pick up the dough and stretch it into a long strand until it begins to tear. Put it on a work surface and then loosely roll it up into a lumpy mass. Knead a few strokes.

Repeat the stretching, rolling, and kneading process until the dough is separating into stringy strands when stretched. Finish by loosely rolling it into a lumpy mass on a work surface. The goal of this technique is to isolate the strands of gluten, which in turn will create the proper beaf texture. Shape into medallions, cutlets, or bites (see page 57).

Beaf Simmering Broth

Beaf simmering broth is used for simmering Basic Beaf Dough (page 55) as part of the preparation process. It can also be used as a savory base for preparing brown sauces, gravies, "jus," hearty soups, and stews. Alternatively, it can be used in any recipe calling for seasoned beef broth. Additional herbs and spices can be included to accommodate specific regional cuisines.

12 cups **water**

3 large **onions**, peeled and quartered

3 ribs **celery**, chopped

1 large **carrot**, unpeeled and chopped

6 cloves **garlic**, crushed

½ cup **tamari**, **soy sauce**, or **Bragg Liquid Aminos**

2 tablespoons **mushroom powder**

2 tablespoons **nutritional yeast flakes**

1 tablespoon **dark brown sugar**

1 tablespoon **Worcestershire Sauce** (page 182) or commercial vegan equivalent

1 teaspoon **sea salt** or **kosher salt**

1 teaspoon whole **black peppercorns**

1 **bay leaf**

Small handful **parsley stems**

Put all the ingredients in a large pot, cover, and simmer over medium-low heat for 1 hour. Season with additional salt to taste. Remove the larger solids with a slotted spoon before adding the beaf.

After simmering the beaf, let the broth cool, then strain it into a sealable container to remove any remaining solids, and refrigerate. During this time, any sediment from the seasonings will settle on the bottom of the container.

The broth can be refrigerated for 1 week or frozen for up to 3 months. To use, decant the clear portion and discard the fine sediment. Be sure to add back water as necessary before using, since the broth will have become concentrated from evaporation during simmering.

If you're using the broth immediately for other purposes, such as soups or stews, strain it through a fine sieve into a clean pot and discard the solids.

QUICK BROTH ALTERNATIVE: Homemade broth is always best and recommended. However, for the sake of convenience and expediency, a quick beaf simmering broth can be made with commercial low-sodium vegetable stock or broth plus 2 teaspoons tamari, soy sauce, or Bragg Liquid Aminos (add more or less to taste) for each cup of stock or broth.

Steak Medallions, Cutlets, or Bites

Basic Beaf Dough is cut into thick medallions, pressed into thin steak cutlets, or torn into small bite-sized nuggets. The medallions, cutlets, or nuggets are partially baked and then simmered in a hearty broth to complete the cooking process. Sorry, pressure cooking is not an alternative to baking the dough; an oven is required.

> **Basic Beaf Dough** (page 55)
> 12 cups **Beaf Simmering Broth** (page 56)

Put a stainless-steel cooling rack on a baking sheet and line the rack with parchment paper or a silicone baking mat. The cooling rack is not required, but it is recommended because it will prevent the excessive browning that would occur from direct contact with the hot baking sheet. Preheat the oven to 350 degrees F (175 degrees C).

Form the dough into medallions, cutlets, or bites (see page 58) and arrange in a single layer on the parchment paper or baking mat. Put the baking sheet on the middle oven rack and bake uncovered for 20 minutes for steak bites, 25 minutes for steak cutlets, or 30 minutes for medallions. Remove from the oven. The beaf will form a dry crust while baking. This is normal and will disappear when the beaf is simmered.

Bring the broth to a boil. If the broth was made from scratch, use a slotted spoon to remove the larger solids. It's not necessary to strain the broth completely until later.

The beaf will be soft at this stage, so handle it carefully. Lower the pieces into the boiling broth and immediately decrease the heat to maintain a gentle simmer. Cook uncovered for 20 minutes for steak bites and cutlets and 30 minutes for medallions; do not boil. Turn the pieces occasionally once they float to the top of the pot to ensure even cooking. When the beaf is done simmering, remove the pot from the heat, cover, and let the beaf cool in the broth.

Transfer the beaf to a food storage bag, seal, and refrigerate for 8 hours to optimize the texture before finishing. Add a marinade at this time if desired.

Strain the cooled broth into a sealable container and refrigerate for future use. The medallions, cutlets, and steak bites are now ready to be finished or used in recipes as desired.

How to Shape Beaf Dough

MEDALLIONS: Stretch and shape the Basic Beaf Dough roughly into a log about 8 inches long. Don't try to smooth the surface, as bumps and irregularities will yield a better finished texture and appearance. Cut the log into 4 equal pieces using a sharp knife. Arrange the pieces cut-side-up/down on the parchment paper or baking mat.

CUTLETS: Slice the Basic Beaf Dough into 6 equal pieces using a sharp knife. Press and stretch each piece against a work surface and shape into a thin cutlet. If the dough is resistant to shaping, let the dough relax a few minutes and then press, stretch, and shape again. Arrange the cutlets in a single layer on the parchment paper or baking mat.

BITES: Slice the dough into 4 equal pieces using a sharp knife. Tear each piece into 6 relatively equal nuggets and arrange them in a single layer on the parchment paper or baking mat. (Note: Tearing the dough yields a better finished texture than slicing.)

Finishing Steak Medallions, Cutlets, or Bites

Medallions can be finished by pan-glazing in a skillet to seal in the juices and create a flavorful brown crust, pan browning and serving "au jus" or with a sauce, or simply smothering them in sautéed mushrooms and onions. Cutlets can be breaded and fried (chikun-fried steak) or sliced into strips, which are ideal for fajitas and stir-fries. Steak Bites can be seasoned or marinated according to the specific dish being prepared. They can then be finished by pan-glazing in a skillet and served as an appetizer or marinated and threaded onto skewers for the grill.

Pan-Glazed Steak Medallions or Bites

YIELDS 4 MEDALLIONS OR 24 BITES

S teak Bites make quick and delicious hors d'oeuvres, while medallions are wonderful for entrées or, when thinly sliced, for sandwich fillings. Pan-glazing is a technique I created to finish these forms of beaf and give them a flavorful brown crust.

2 tablespoons **dry red wine**

2 teaspoons **Worcestershire Sauce** (page 182) or commercial vegan equivalent

2 tablespoons **nondairy butter** or **margarine**

4 prepared **Steak Medallions**, or 24 prepared **Steak Bites** (page 57)

Freshly ground **black pepper**

Chopped **fresh parsley**

Put the wine and Worcestershire Sauce in a small dish and set aside.

Put the butter in a nonstick skillet over medium heat until melted. Add the steak medallions or bites and sauté, turning occasionally, until coated in the sizzling butter. Add the wine mixture, and continue to sauté until most of the liquid has evaporated and the beaf is nicely browned. Season with pepper to taste. Be sure to run a stove exhaust fan while pan-glazing, as some smoke will be produced.

For medallions, transfer to individual serving plates and garnish with parsley. For steak bites, transfer to a serving platter, insert toothpicks, and garnish with parsley.

Steak en Brochette (SHISH KEBAB)

S teak Bites have a high moisture content and a tender texture, which makes them ideal for skewering and grilling. *En brochette* is the French term (*shish kebab* or *shish kabob* is the Middle Eastern term) for skewered and grilled chunks of meat, with or without vegetables. This recipe makes mini appetizer skewers or dinner skewers. *NOTE: The Steak Bites need to marinate in the refrigerator for 8 to 12 hours before grilling, so plan accordingly.*

24 prepared **Steak Bites** (page 57)

Marinade of choice

Kebab vegetables (such as bell pepper, eggplant, cherry tomatoes, onion chunks, mushrooms, or zucchini), **cut in thick, bite-sized pieces** (for dinner skewers only)

Pineapple chunks (for dinner skewers only; optional)

Put the Steak Bites in a medium bowl, cover with the marinade, and refrigerate for 8 to 12 hours.

For mini appetizer skewers, soak ten 6-inch bamboo skewers in water for several hours to discourage the wood from burning. Cut or tear the Steak Bites into smaller pieces before skewering.

For dinner skewers, soak 4 full-sized bamboo skewers in water for several hours to discourage the wood from burning. Skewer the Steak Bites alternating with your choice of kebab vegetables and optional pineapple.

For pan grilling, oil a nonstick grill pan. For outdoor grilling, brush or spray the grill grates with cooking oil or use a nonstick grill mat. Brush the Steak Bites with cooking oil before broiling or outdoor grilling, then continue to brush them generously and frequently with marinade while broiling or grilling to keep the beaf moist and tender.

Steak en Brochette (Shish Kebab)

Steak Diane

 teak Diane consists of tender Steak Medallions flambéed and served with a rich mushroom, shallot, and cognac cream sauce.

4 prepared **Steak Medallions** (page 57)

Coarsely ground **black pepper**

2 tablespoons **olive oil**, plus more as needed

1 small **shallot**, finely chopped

1 cup sliced **cremini or white mushrooms**

Sea salt or **kosher salt**

2 cloves **garlic**, minced

2 tablespoons **nondairy butter** or **margarine**

1 tablespoon **Worcestershire Sauce** (page 182) or commercial vegan equivalent

1 tablespoon **Dijon mustard**

⅓ cup **brandy** or **cognac**

1 cup **Soy Cream** (page 187) or **Light Cashew Cream** (page 189)

¼ cup chopped **fresh parsley**, lightly packed

Let the medallions come to room temperature for 30 minutes before proceeding.

Season the medallions on both sides with pepper. Put the oil in a large non-stick skillet over medium heat. Pan sear the medallions until lightly browned on both sides. Transfer to a plate and cover to keep warm until the sauce is prepared. Do not wipe or clean the skillet.

If the skillet is dry, add an additional tablespoon of oil. Add the shallot and sauté over medium heat until softened. Add the mushrooms and a pinch of salt. Sauté until the mushrooms have released their moisture and are beginning to lightly brown. Add the garlic and sauté for 1 minute. Add the butter and stir until melted. Stir in the Worcestershire Sauce and mustard and heat for 30 seconds.

Briefly remove the skillet from the heat and add the cognac. Put the skillet back over the heat and carefully ignite the alcohol with a long match or long-stemmed butane lighter (see Tips from Chef Skye, below). Shake the skillet gently until the flames die.

Stir in the cream and allow the sauce to thicken slightly before decreasing the heat to medium-low. Add the medallions and 2 tablespoons of the parsley and cook briefly until heated through, about 1 minute.

Arrange the medallions on individual serving plates. Spoon the sauce over the medallions and sprinkle with the remaining parsley.

Tips from Chef Skye ▪ Exercise extreme caution when igniting the alcohol as it will produce a rather dramatic flame. Hold the skillet away from your body and away from anything flammable, such as kitchen curtains.

Steak Medici

 teak Medici consists of tender Steak Medallions pan seared and served with sautéed mushrooms in a port wine glaze.

4 prepared **Steak Medallions** (page 57)

2 tablespoons **olive oil**, plus more as needed

1 cup sliced **cremini or white mushrooms**

Sea salt or **kosher salt**

2 tablespoons **nondairy butter** or **margarine**

½ cup **port wine**

¼ cup chopped **fresh parsley**, lightly packed

Let the medallions come to room temperature for 30 minutes before proceeding.

Put the oil in a large nonstick skillet over medium heat. Pan sear the medallions until lightly browned on both sides. Transfer to a plate and cover to keep warm until the sauce is prepared. Do not wipe or clean the skillet.

If the skillet is dry, add an additional tablespoon of oil. Add the mushrooms and a pinch salt. Sauté until the mushrooms have released their moisture and are beginning to lightly brown. Add the butter and stir until melted. Add the medallions, port wine, and 2 tablespoons of the parsley and cook briefly until heated through, about 1 minute.

Arrange the medallions on individual serving plates. Spoon the mushrooms and sauce around the medallions and garnish with the remaining parsley.

Steak au Poivre

ender Steak Medallions are encrusted with cracked black pepper, pan seared until nicely browned, and topped with a cognac cream sauce flavored with mustard and thyme.

4 prepared **Steak Medallions** (page 57)

⅔ cup **Soy Cream** (page 187) or **Light Cashew Cream** (page 189)

⅓ cup **Beaf Simmering Broth** (page 56)

2 teaspoons **Dijon mustard**

½ teaspoon **dried thyme**

1 tablespoon cracked **black pepper**, plus more as needed

2 tablespoons **olive oil**, plus more as needed

1 small **shallot**, finely chopped

2 tablespoons **nondairy butter** or **margarine**

⅓ cup **cognac** or **brandy**

Let the medallions come to room temperature for 30 minutes before proceeding.

Put the cream, broth, mustard, and thyme in a small bowl and whisk to combine. Set aside.

Scatter the pepper on a plate and press the medallions into the pepper. Use more pepper as needed.

Put the oil in a large nonstick skillet over medium heat. Pan sear the medallions until lightly browned. Transfer to a plate and cover to keep warm until the sauce is prepared. Do not wipe or clean the skillet.

If the skillet is dry, add an additional tablespoon of oil. Add the shallot and sauté until translucent. Add the butter or margarine and stir until melted.

Put the skillet back over the heat and carefully ignite the alcohol with a long match or long-stemmed butane lighter (see Tips from Chef Skye, page 63). Shake the skillet gently until the flames die.

Stir in the reserved cream mixture and cook until the sauce has slightly thickened. Remove from the heat.

Arrange the medallions on individual serving plates. Pour the sauce over the medallions and serve immediately.

Beaf Kushiyaki (JAPANESE SKEWERED GRILLED BEAF)

ender beaf Steak Bites are marinated in a sweet-and-savory tamari-based sauce before being skewered and grilled. For this recipe, you will need four bamboo skewers.

MARINADE

½ cup **Japanese sake** or **mirin** (Japanese sweet rice wine), or ½ cup **water** with 1 tablespoon **rice vinegar**

¼ cup **tamari**, **soy sauce**, or **Bragg Liquid Aminos**

¼ cup **dark brown sugar**

1 tablespoon **cooking oil**, plus additional for grilling

2 teaspoons **Worcestershire Sauce** (page 182) or commercial vegan equivalent

5 cloves **garlic**

1 teaspoon toasted **sesame oil**

½ teaspoon crushed **red pepper flakes**

STEAK BITES

24 prepared **Steak Bites** (page 57)

Chopped **scallions**, for garnish

Soak 4 bamboo skewers in water for several hours before grilling to discourage the wood from burning.

Put all the marinade ingredients in a blender and process until smooth. Pour into a food storage bag and add the Steak Bites. Press the air out of the bag, seal, and refrigerate for 8 to 12 hours before grilling or broiling.

Thread the marinated beaf on the bamboo skewers. The skewers can be broiled or grilled. For grilling, brush or spray a nonstick grill pan or outdoor grill grates with cooking oil. Brush the beaf with cooking oil and then grill or broil, turning occasionally, until lightly browned. Generously and frequently brush the beaf with the marinade while grilling or broiling to keep it moist and tender. Avoid overcooking. Garnish with chopped scallions before serving.

Prime Cut Roast Beaf WITH QUICK PAN GRAVY

T ender Prime Cut Roast Beaf slices are delicious served "au jus," with Quick Pan Gravy, or with a favorite sauce. Leftovers are superb for hot or cold deli-style sandwiches too. Sorry, pressure cooking is not an alternative to baking the dough; an oven is required. *NOTE: The prepared Roast Beaf must be refrigerated for 8 hours prior to finishing to optimize its texture, so plan accordingly.*

ROAST BEAF

Basic Beaf Dough (page 55)

12 cups **Beaf Simmering Broth** (page 56)

PAN-GLAZING

2 tablespoons **dry red wine** or **dry sherry** or **additional broth**

2 teaspoons **Worcestershire Sauce** (page 182) or commercial vegan equivalent

2 tablespoons **nondairy butter** or **margarine**

½ teaspoon coarsely ground **black pepper**

Ground spices and fresh or dried **herbs** of choice (optional)

QUICK PAN GRAVY (OPTIONAL)

4 tablespoons **nondairy butter** or **margarine**

¼ cup **all-purpose flour**

2 cups **Beaf Simmering Broth** (reserved from preparing the Roast Beaf)

¾ teaspoon **browning liquid** (color enhancer)

Sea salt or **kosher salt**

Freshly ground **black pepper**

Put a stainless-steel cooling rack on a baking sheet and line the rack with parchment paper or a silicone baking mat. The cooling rack is not required, but it is recommended because it will prevent the excessive browning that would occur from direct contact with the hot baking sheet. Preheat the oven to 350 degrees F (175 degrees C).

Form the Basic Beaf Dough into a thick, compact slab. Don't worry about smoothing the surface too much, as some bumps and irregularities will yield a more natural finished appearance. Transfer the dough to the parchment paper or baking mat.

Put the baking sheet on the middle oven rack, bake uncovered for 45 minutes, and then remove from the oven. The roast will form a dry crust while baking. This is normal and will disappear when the roast is simmered.

Bring the broth to a boil. If the broth was made from scratch, use a slotted spoon to remove the larger solids. It's not necessary to strain the broth completely until later.

Carefully lower the roast into the boiling broth and immediately decrease the heat to maintain a gentle simmer. Cook uncovered for 45 minutes. Monitor the pot frequently to make sure the broth is maintained at a simmer; do not boil. Turn the roast occasionally in the broth as it simmers to ensure even cooking. After simmering, remove the pot from the heat, cover, and let the roast cool in the broth.

Transfer the roast to a food storage bag, seal, and refrigerate for 8 hours to optimize the texture before finishing. Add a marinade at this time if desired. Strain the cooled broth into a sealable container and refrigerate for future use. *NOTE: You will need 2 cups of the broth to make the optional Quick Pan Gravy.*

To pan-glaze the roast, bring it to room temperature 1 hour before finishing. Put the wine and Worcestershire Sauce in a small dish and set aside.

Put the butter in a large, deep nonstick skillet over medium heat until melted. Add the roast and turn until it is coated all over with the butter. Lightly brown the roast, turning it frequently. Add the wine mixture. The mixture will sizzle and the sugars in it will begin to caramelize, turning the roast a beautiful deep-brown color. Be sure to run a stove exhaust fan while pan-glazing, as some smoke will be produced.

Add the pepper and any optional spices and herbs and continue to turn the roast in the mixture to form a crust. Transfer to a serving platter and slice.

To make the pan gravy, put the butter in a large, deep nonstick skillet over medium heat until melted. Sprinkle in the flour and stir to form a thick paste (roux). Cook the roux until it emits a nutty aroma, 1 to 2 minutes.

Incorporate the Beaf Simmering Broth in small increments, whisking vigorously until smooth after each addition of broth. Continue to whisk, loosening any browned bits of glaze stuck to the skillet as you stir (this process is known as *deglazing*). Add the browning liquid to enrich the color.

Increase the heat to medium-high and cook, stirring frequently, until the mixture is bubbling and begins to thicken. Season with salt and pepper to taste. Decrease the heat to low to keep warm until ready to serve, stirring occasionally.

Tips from Chef Skye ■ If pan-glazing has not sufficiently reheated the roast, preheat the oven to 350 degrees F (175 degrees C). Put the roast in a shallow baking dish, cover with foil, and bake for 20 minutes.

Sauerbraten

I n German, *sauerbraten* means "sour roast." Actually, the roast and gravy boast a wonderful combination of sweet-and-sour flavors. Serve with German red cabbage and potatoes of choice or spätzle. *Wunderbar! NOTE: The roast requires 8 hours for marinating, so plan accordingly.*

ROAST BEAF

Prime Cut Roast Beaf (page 68), simmered and cooled in the broth

Chopped **fresh parsley**, for garnish

MARINADE

¼ cup **Beaf Simmering Broth** (page 56)

¼ cup **red wine vinegar** or **apple cider vinegar**

GRAVY

¼ cup **nondairy butter** or **margarine**

¼ cup **all-purpose flour**

4 cups **Beaf Simmering Broth** (reserved from preparing the Roast Beaf)

1 large **onion**, peeled and chopped

1 large **carrot**, unpeeled and chopped

¼ cup **seedless raisins**

2 tablespoons **dark brown sugar**

12 **juniper berries** (optional)

1 teaspoon **Dijon mustard**

1 teaspoon **ground ginger**

½ teaspoon **ground cloves**

½ teaspoon ground **black pepper**

1 **bay leaf**

Sea salt or **kosher salt**

The day before serving, prepare the Roast Beaf. Let the roast cool in the simmering broth and then transfer to a food storage bag. Add the marinade ingredients to the bag, seal, and refrigerate for 8 hours.

Strain the remaining cooled broth into a sealable container and refrigerate for future use. (You will need 4 cups of the broth for the gravy.)

Bring the roast to room temperature for 1 hour. Drain the marinade from the bag and reserve it for the gravy.

Preheat the oven to 250 degrees F (120 degrees C). Spray a large nonstick skillet with cooking oil and place over medium heat. Brown the roast on both sides in the hot skillet. Transfer to a heatproof plate or shallow baking dish, cover with foil, and put in the oven to keep warm while the gravy is prepared.

To make the gravy, put the butter in a large pot over medium heat until melted. Sprinkle in the flour and stir to create a thick paste (roux). Cook until the roux emits a nutty aroma, 1 to 2 minutes.

Incorporate the beaf broth in small increments while whisking vigorously until smooth after each addition of broth. Add the reserved marinade, onion, carrot, raisins, brown sugar, optional juniper berries, mustard, ginger, cloves, pepper, and bay leaf. Bring to a boil over medium-high heat, stirring frequently. Decrease the heat to maintain a simmer, partially cover the pot, and cook for 45 minutes, stirring occasionally. Season with salt to taste.

Remove the roast from the oven and thinly slice. Transfer to a serving platter.

Press the gravy through a sieve and discard the solids. Generously ladle the gravy over the sliced sauerbraten and garnish with chopped parsley. Pour the remaining gravy into a gravy boat to serve on the side. Serve immediately.

Beaf Brisket

Beaf Brisket is formulated differently from the other beaf analogue recipes in order to produce a pull-apart texture that is remarkably similar to beef that has been slow-simmered for hours. It is ideal for Classic Pot Roast (page 83), but it can also be shredded or diced and used in stews, soups, pot pies, hot wraps or sandwiches, stir-fries, flash sautés, and Mexican cuisine. A pressure cooker is recommended for preparation; however, oven baking is an option. A food processor is required for this recipe to achieve the proper finished texture. If you have a large-capacity food processor, see page 42.

1½ cups (225 g) **vital wheat gluten**

5 ounces (142 g) extra-firm block **tofu**, pressed (see page 11)

1 cup (240 ml) **water**

3 tablespoons **tamari**, **soy sauce**, or **Bragg Liquid Aminos**

2 tablespoons **olive oil**

2 tablespoons **mushroom powder**

4 teaspoons **onion powder**

2 teaspoons **garlic powder**

2 teaspoons **Worcestershire Sauce** (page 182) or commercial vegan equivalent

2 teaspoons **browning liquid** (color enhancer)

1 tablespoon **dry rub seasoning** of choice (optional)

Put the vital wheat gluten in a large bowl. Set aside.

Crumble the tofu into a blender. Add the water, tamari, oil, mushroom powder, onion powder, garlic powder, Worcestershire Sauce, and browning liquid. Process until smooth and creamy, stopping the blender as necessary to scrape down the jar.

Scoop the tofu mixture into the vital wheat gluten and combine with a sturdy silicone spatula until the tofu mixture is incorporated and a sticky ball of dough begins to form.

Put the dough in a food processor fitted with a standard chopping blade or plastic dough blade and process for 2 minutes. If you have a small-capacity food processor, divide the dough in half and process each half separately to reduce wear and tear on the motor.

The processor may bounce as the dough reaches its desired elasticity. If it does, simply hold the processor in place. The dough, when sufficiently processed, should be sticky, stretchy, glossy, and slightly warm. Occasionally, the sticky dough may creep up onto the motor shaft of the processor during processing. Simply clean it up with a damp paper towel.

To wrap the dough, lay an 18-inch-long sheet of heavy-duty aluminum foil on a work surface. Transfer the dough to the foil and shape into a compact mass. If you are using a dry rub seasoning, sprinkle 1 tablespoon of the mixture over the dough. Roll the mass of dough in the foil and twist the ends tightly to seal. Bend the ends in half to lock them tight. Wrap the package in a second sheet of foil in a similar manner.

If you will be oven baking the dough (rather than pressure cooking it), twist the ends of the foil tightly but leave a small amount of air space in the package on each side to allow for expansion of the dough during baking. Wrap it in a third sheet of foil for reinforcement.

To pressure cook, put 3 cups of water in the cooker and put the trivet in place. Add the package, seal the lid, close the steam valve, and cook on high for 1 hour and 30 minutes. Turn the unit off and let the pressure release naturally for 30 minutes. Remove the package from the cooker and let cool until it can be handled comfortably.

To oven bake (instead of pressure cook), preheat the oven to 350 degrees F (175 degrees C). Put the foil package directly on the middle oven rack and bake for 2 hours. Remove from the oven and let cool until the package can be handled comfortably.

For Classic Pot Roast (page 83), refrigerate the foil package for 8 hours to optimize the texture. Leave the roast intact and proceed with the recipe.

To shred the brisket, bend the warm roast in half to split it lengthwise and reveal the "grain." Tear the roast in half following the split. Bend and tear those pieces in half lengthwise. Pull the brisket into long strips, following the grain as much as possible. Tear those pieces into chunks or smaller bite-sized pieces. Alternatively, the pieces can be diced or cubed. Refrigerate the shredded or diced brisket for 8 hours to optimize its texture before using in recipes.

Tips from Chef Skye

- For pot pies and saucy casseroles, mix the shredded or diced brisket with the other ingredients before baking.

- For soups and stews, add the shredded or diced brisket during the last 20 minutes of cooking time before serving.

Spicy Thai Beaf Salad

ssorted greens, bean sprouts, cucumber, scallions, red onion, cilantro, and mint are topped with freshly pan-grilled beef and then dressed with a spicy, peppery tamari-lime dressing.

TAMARI-LIME DRESSING

⅓ cup freshly squeezed **lime juice** (about 3 limes)

3 tablespoons **tamari**, **soy sauce**, or **Bragg Liquid Aminos**

2 tablespoons **peanut oil** or **olive oil**

1 tablespoon seeded and minced fresh **Thai, serrano, or jalapeño chile**

1 tablespoon **organic sugar**

1 tablespoon finely chopped **fresh mint**

BEAF SALAD

8 cups assorted chopped **salad greens**

½ medium **red onion**, thinly sliced

1 large **cucumber**, peeled, halved lengthwise, seeded, and cut into ¼-inch slices

1 handful **fresh bean sprouts**

2 **scallions**, chopped

¼ cup chopped **fresh cilantro**, lightly packed

2 tablespoons **olive oil**

12 ounces prepared **Prime Cut Roast Beef** (page 68), thinly sliced

Dash **tamari**, **soy sauce**, or **Bragg Liquid Aminos**

½ teaspoon coarsely ground **black pepper**

¼ cup **unsalted peanuts**, coarsely chopped

To make the dressing, put the lime juice, tamari, oil, chile, and sugar in a small bowl and whisk until the sugar is dissolved. Stir in the mint and set aside.

To make the salad, put the greens, onion, cucumber, bean sprouts, scallions, and cilantro in a large bowl. Set aside.

To prepare the beaf, put the oil in a large skillet over medium-high heat until hot but not smoking. Pan sear the beaf until lightly browned. Season with a dash of tamari and the pepper while pan searing. Remove from the heat and let cool for 5 minutes.

Add the beaf to the salad. Drizzle with the dressing and toss. Sprinkle with the peanuts and serve.

Chinese Pepper Beaf

T ender sliced beaf, bell pepper, onion, and garlic are stir-fried and tossed in a savory tamari-based sauce. Serve it over steamed rice.

¾ cup **water**

¼ cup **tamari**, **soy sauce**, or **Bragg Liquid Aminos**

2 teaspoons **dark brown sugar**

2 tablespoons **cooking oil**

12 ounces prepared **Prime Cut Roast Beaf** (page 68), thinly sliced and cut
    into bite-sized pieces

1 large **white or yellow onion**, chopped

1 **green bell pepper**, cut into bite-sized pieces

1 **red bell pepper**, cut into bite-sized pieces

3 cloves **garlic**, thinly sliced

1 tablespoon grated **fresh ginger** (see page 31)

½ teaspoon crushed **red pepper flakes**

1 tablespoon **unmodified potato starch** or **cornstarch**

Put the water, tamari, and brown sugar in a bowl or measuring cup and stir to combine. Set aside.

Put 1 tablespoon of the oil in a nonstick wok or deep skillet over medium heat. Brown the beaf in the skillet. Transfer to a plate and set aside.

Put the remaining tablespoon of oil in the wok, add the onion, green bell pepper, and red bell pepper and sauté until the onion is golden, about 5 minutes. Add the garlic, ginger, and red pepper flakes and sauté for 1 minute.

Stir in the tamari mixture, bring to a simmer, cover, and cook for 5 minutes.

While the vegetables are cooking, create a slurry by mixing the starch with 1 tablespoon of water in a small dish until dissolved. Stir the slurry into the vegetables and cook uncovered until the mixture begins to thicken. Add the beaf slices and toss gently to combine and heat through. Serve hot.

Beaf Crumbles

Beaf crumbles can be used in any recipe calling for cooked and crumbled ground beef, such as pasta with "meat" sauce, chili, casseroles, Mexican cuisine, and so forth. For this application, Basic Beaf Dough is wrapped in foil and steamed until partially cooked. The beaf is then ground in a food processor, seasoned as desired, and lightly browned in a skillet to finish cooking. Beaf Crumbles can be prepared in a pressure cooker or conventional steamer.

Basic Beaf Dough (page 55)
2 tablespoons **olive oil**
1 medium **onion**, finely diced
3 cloves **garlic**, minced
Fresh or dried **herbs and spices** (optional)
Sea salt or **kosher salt**
Coarsely ground **black pepper**

Lay an 18-inch-long sheet of heavy-duty aluminum foil on a work surface. Put the dough on the foil and form into a slab. Fold the dough in the foil to create a flattened package. Fold in the ends and crimp the edges to seal. Wrap with a second sheet of foil in a similar manner.

To pressure cook, put 3 cups of water in the cooker and put the trivet in place. Add the package, seal the lid, close the steam valve, and cook on high for 15 minutes. Turn the unit off and let the steam release naturally for 30 minutes. Remove the package and let cool for 1 hour.

To steam (instead of pressure cook), put a steamer insert into a pot and add enough water to just reach the bottom of it. Bring the water to a rapid boil over high heat and add the foil package. Cover the pot and steam for 45 minutes. Check the pot occasionally and add hot water as necessary to replace the water lost to steam evaporation. Remove the package and let cool for 1 hour.

Refrigerate for 8 hours to optimize the texture before finishing.

To finish, cut the beaf into chunks and transfer to a food processor fitted with a standard chopping blade. Grind the beaf to the desired texture. Use immediately or transfer to a food storage bag, seal, and refrigerate until ready to use.

To brown the crumbles, put the oil in a large skillet over medium heat. Add the onion and sauté until tender, about 5 minutes. Add the garlic and any optional herbs and spices of your choice and sauté for 1 minute. Add the crumbled beaf, mix well, and cook, stirring frequently, until the crumbles are lightly browned. Season with salt and pepper to taste. Use in recipes as desired.

Classic Pot Roast

With its chunks of tender vegan beef, onions, potatoes, carrots, garlic, herbs, and a luscious gravy, Classic Pot Roast is at once rustic, delicious, and comforting. Serve it with prepared horseradish if desired. Leftover pot roast and gravy are superb reheated for open-faced sandwiches.

¼ cup **olive oil**

¼ cup **all-purpose flour**

4 cups **Beaf Simmering Broth** (page 56)

¼ cup **dry red wine** (such as Cabernet Sauvignon or Merlot; optional)

1 prepared **Beaf Brisket** (page 74)

3 large **carrots**, peeled and cut into chunks

2 large **yellow onions**, cut into chunks

2 large **russet potatoes**, peeled and cut into chunks

3 cloves **garlic**, minced

3 sprigs **fresh thyme**, or ¾ teaspoon dried thyme

1 sprig **fresh rosemary** (optional)

Sea salt or **kosher salt**

Coarsely ground **black pepper**

Browning liquid (color enhancer; optional)

Chopped **fresh parsley**, for garnish

Put the oil in a large pot over medium heat. Add the flour and stir to create a paste (roux). Cook until the flour emits a nutty aroma, about 2 minutes. Incorporate the broth in small increments while vigorously whisking the mixture until smooth. Stir in the optional wine.

Bend the brisket lengthwise until it splits; this will allow the gravy to penetrate the roast. Add the brisket, carrots, onions, potatoes, garlic, thyme, and rosemary to the pot. Increase the heat slightly to bring to a boil, partially cover the pot, and decrease the heat to just above low. Let the vegetables cook until very tender, about 45 minutes.

Season with salt and pepper to taste. To enhance the color of the gravy, add optional browning liquid in small amounts to achieve the desired color.

Remove the fresh rosemary and thyme stems and discard. Transfer the roast to a serving platter and shred with a fork. Arrange the vegetables around the roast using a slotted spoon. Ladle some of the gravy over the roast and vegetables. Garnish with chopped parsley.

Corned Beaf

Corned Beaf is delicious any time of the year, but it's especially appropriate for celebrating St. Patrick's Day. This recipe requires time for marinating and chilling the brisket, so begin the preparation a day ahead or at least early in the day you're planning to serve it. This is a large roast, which allows it to be served as an entrée with ample leftovers for sandwiches. Serve it warm with grainy mustard, prepared horseradish, or Horsey Sauce (page 175). A pressure cooker is recommended for preparation; however, oven baking is an option.

AROMATIC BRINE

12 cups **water**	1 teaspoon whole **black peppercorns**
2 tablespoons **sea salt** or **kosher salt**	1 teaspoon whole **coriander seeds**
2 tablespoons **organic sugar**	1 teaspoon **caraway seeds**
1 teaspoon whole **cloves**	1 (1-inch) piece **fresh ginger**, sliced
1 teaspoon whole **allspice berries**	½ **cinnamon stick**
1 teaspoon whole **juniper berries**, lightly crushed	¼ teaspoon **yellow mustard seeds**
2 **bay leaves**	

DRY INGREDIENTS

2 cups (300 g) **vital wheat gluten**	2 tablespoons **onion powder**
¼ cup **garbanzo bean flour**	1 tablespoon **garlic powder**

LIQUID INGREDIENTS

1¾ cups (420 ml) **water**	2 tablespoons neutral **vegetable oil**
2 tablespoons **tamari**, **soy sauce**, or **Bragg Liquid Aminos**	1 teaspoon **sea salt** or **kosher salt**

BRINE COLORING

2 cups (480 ml) cooled **aromatic brine**	1 tablespoon **beet powder**

Put all the aromatic brine ingredients in a large pot. Cover and bring to a boil over medium-high heat. Decrease the heat to medium-low and simmer gently for 20 minutes. Remove from the heat and let cool for a few hours.

While the brine is cooling, prepare and cook the brisket. Put all the dry ingredients in a large bowl and whisk to combine. Put the liquid ingredients in a small bowl or measuring cup and stir until the salt dissolves.

Pour the liquid ingredients (not the aromatic brine or brine coloring) into the dry ingredients and combine thoroughly to develop the gluten. Knead the dough in the bowl until it feels elastic, about 2 minutes.

Lay an 18-inch-long sheet of heavy-duty foil on a work surface. Put the dough on the foil and flatten it into a slab about 1 inch thick. Flat wrap the dough in the foil (don't roll it), folding it over several times to create a flattened package. Fold in the ends and crimp to seal the foil. Put the package on a second sheet of foil and wrap it in a similar manner. If you will be oven baking the dough (rather than pressure cooking it), wrap it in a third sheet of foil for reinforcement.

To pressure cook, put 3 cups of water in the cooker and put the trivet in place. Add the package, seal the lid, close the steam valve, and cook on high for 1 hour and 45 minutes. Turn the unit off and let the pressure release naturally for 30 minutes. Remove the package from the cooker and let cool until it can be handled comfortably.

To oven bake (instead of pressure cook), preheat the oven to 350 degrees F (175 degrees C). Put the foil package directly on the middle oven rack and bake for 2 hours. Remove from the oven and let cool until the package can be handled comfortably.

While the package is cooling, prepare the brine coloring. Strain the aromatic brine to remove and discard the spice solids. Reserve all of the brine (it will be needed for coloring and heating the brisket).

Put the beet powder in a medium bowl. Add 2 cups of the brine and stir until completely dissolved.

Unwrap the brisket and put it on a cutting board. With a sharp knife, trim away the thin layer of dry crust from the ends of the brisket and discard. Slice the brisket in half and trim away the thin layer of crust from the broad sides of the brisket and discard. Slice the brisket as thinly as possible, then transfer the slices to a food storage bag.

Pour the brine coloring mixture into the food storage bag. Seal and turn the bag repeatedly to coat the slices with the mixture. Refrigerate for 8 to 12 hours to marinate and stain with color.

To heat and serve the brisket, pour the remaining aromatic brine into a large pot and bring to a simmer over medium heat. Remove from the heat. Drain and discard the brine coloring mixture and transfer the beaf slices to the hot brine. Cover and let stand for 10 minutes (in addition to reheating the beaf, this will help to remove any excess color).

Remove the beaf slices with a slotted spoon and transfer to a serving platter. Discard the brine.

Tips from Chef Skye

- If you want to cook cabbage in the aromatic brine, cook and remove it before adding the color-infused brisket; otherwise, the cabbage will be stained by the beet color.

- To reheat leftover Corned Beaf, wrap the slices securely in foil and put in a preheated oven at 350 degrees F (175 degrees C) or in a steamer for 20 minutes. Alternatively, the slices can be gently reheated in a lightly oiled skillet over medium-low heat.

VARIATION: Replace all the spices in the aromatic brine with 2 tablespoons commercial pickling spice blend plus 1 teaspoon caraway seeds.

Deli-Style Pastrami

My signature meatless pastrami captures all the taste, texture, and appearance of real pastrami without the animal cruelty or grisly fat. It has a smoky flavor and is generously seasoned with black pepper and other select spices. A pressure cooker is recommended for preparation; however, oven baking is an option.

DRY INGREDIENTS

1 cup (150 g) **vital wheat gluten**

2 tablespoons **garbanzo bean flour**

1 tablespoon **onion powder**

2 teaspoons **garlic powder**

1 teaspoon **ground coriander**

½ teaspoon **smoked paprika**

½ teaspoon **dry mustard**

¼ teaspoon **ground allspice**

¼ teaspoon **ground cloves**

LIQUID INGREDIENTS

1 cup (240 ml) **water**

2 tablespoons **tamari**, **soy sauce**, or **Bragg Liquid Aminos**

1 tablespoon **olive oil**

ADDITIONAL SEASONING INGREDIENT

1½ teaspoons coarsely ground **black pepper**

BRINE COLORING

1 cup (240 ml) **water**

1 tablespoon **dark brown sugar**

2 teaspoons **hickory liquid smoke**

2 teaspoons **beet powder**

1 teaspoon **sea salt** or **kosher salt**

To make the dough, put the dry ingredients in a large bowl and whisk to combine. Put the liquid ingredients in a small bowl or measuring cup and stir to combine. Pour into the dry ingredients and combine thoroughly to develop the gluten. Knead the dough in the bowl until it feels elastic, about 1 minute.

Lay an 18-inch-long sheet of heavy-duty foil on a work surface. Put the dough on the foil and flatten it into a slab about 1 inch thick. Sprinkle the surface of the dough with half of the black pepper. Flip the slab over and repeat with the remaining pepper.

Flat wrap the dough in the foil (don't roll it), folding over several times to create a flattened package. Fold in the ends and crimp to seal the foil. Put the package on a second sheet of foil and wrap in a similar manner. If you will be oven baking the dough (rather than pressure cooking it), wrap it in a third sheet of foil for reinforcement.

To pressure cook, put 3 cups of water in the cooker and put the trivet in place. Add the package, seal the lid, close the steam valve, and cook on high for 1 hour and 15 minutes. Turn the unit off and let the pressure release naturally for 30 minutes. Remove the package from the cooker and let cool until it can be handled comfortably.

To oven bake (instead of pressure cook), preheat the oven to 350 degrees F (175 degrees C). Put the foil package directly on the middle oven rack and bake for 1 hour and 30 minutes. Remove from the oven and let cool until the package can be handled comfortably.

Slice the pastrami as thinly as possible. Transfer the slices to a food storage bag.

Put the brine coloring ingredients in a small bowl or measuring cup and stir until the sugar, beet powder, and salt dissolve. Pour the brine coloring into the food storage bag. Seal and turn the bag repeatedly to coat the slices with the mixture. Refrigerate for a minimum of 1 hour to marinate and stain with color.

Drain and discard the brine coloring and gently pat the slices with paper towels to remove excess liquid. Lightly coat a nonstick skillet with cooking oil and place over medium-low heat. Gently toss the slices in the skillet until heated through.

Basic Porq Dough

Basic Porq Dough is prepared from a blend of vital wheat gluten, tofu, and select seasonings. The basic dough is used to create chops or cutlets for use in a wide range of recipes. The select seasonings used in the porq dough make it amenable to a variety of applications and cuisines.

1½ cups (225 g) **vital wheat gluten**

5 ounces (142 g) extra-firm block **tofu**, pressed (see page 11)

¾ cup (180 ml) **water**

2 tablespoons neutral **vegetable oil**

2 tablespoons mellow **white miso**

4 teaspoons **onion powder**

1 tablespoon **tamari**, **soy sauce**, or **Bragg Liquid Aminos**

2 teaspoons **garlic powder**

BLENDER METHOD: Put the vital wheat gluten in a large bowl. Set aside.

Crumble the tofu into a blender. Add the water, oil, miso, onion powder, tamari, and garlic powder. Process until smooth and creamy. Stop the blender as necessary to scrape down the jar.

Scoop the tofu mixture into the vital wheat gluten and combine with a sturdy silicone spatula until the tofu mixture is incorporated and a stiff dough begins to form. The mixture may seem a bit dry at first; do not add more water.

Transfer the dough to a clean work surface (do not flour the work surface) and knead vigorously until the dough is springy and elastic, about 2 minutes.

Stretch the dough until it begins to tear, then roll it up into a mass. If it tears too easily, knead for an additional minute or until it can be stretched a bit before tearing. Shape the dough into a compact log and then proceed with making chops or cutlets (see page 94).

FOOD PROCESSOR METHOD: Crumble the tofu into a food processor fitted with a plastic dough blade or standard chopping blade and process into fine crumbles. Add half of the water and the oil, miso, onion powder, tamari, and garlic powder. Process until as smooth as possible. Stop to scrape down the work bowl as needed.

Add the vital wheat gluten with the remaining water. Process for 1 minute. Transfer the dough to a work surface, shape into a compact log, and proceed with making chops or cutlets (see page 94).

Porq Simmering Broth

P orq Simmering Broth is used for simmering Basic Porq Dough (page 92) as part of the preparation process. If you like, additional herbs or spices can be added to accommodate specific regional cuisines.

12 cups **water**

¼ cup **tamari**, **soy sauce**, or **Bragg Liquid Aminos**

3 large **onions**, peeled and quartered

3 ribs **celery**, chopped

2 large **carrots**, unpeeled and chopped

6 cloves **garlic**, crushed

2 tablespoons **nutritional yeast flakes**

2 teaspoons **sea salt** or **kosher salt**

1 teaspoon whole **black peppercorns**

3 sprigs **fresh thyme**, or ½ teaspoon dried thyme

1 **bay leaf**

Small handful **parsley stems**

Put all the ingredients in a large pot, cover, and simmer over medium-low heat for 1 hour. Season with additional salt to taste. Remove the larger solids with a slotted spoon before adding the porq.

After simmering the porq, let the broth cool, then strain it into a sealable container to remove any remaining solids, and refrigerate. During this time, any sediment from the seasonings will settle on the bottom of the container.

The broth can be refrigerated for 1 week or frozen for up to 3 months. To use, decant the clear portion and discard the fine sediment. Be sure to add back water as necessary before using, since the broth will have become concentrated from evaporation during simmering.

If you're using the broth immediately for other purposes, strain it through a fine sieve into a clean pot and discard the solids.

QUICK BROTH ALTERNATIVES: Homemade broth is always best. However, for the sake of convenience and expediency, a quick porq simmering broth can be made with commercial vegetable bouillon paste (1 teaspoon for each cup of water) or vegetable broth cubes (½ cube for each cup of water), more or less to taste. Commercial vegetable broths are also available in aseptic cartons from most markets. Add additional herbs and spices as desired to accommodate specific regional cuisines. Season the prepared broth with salt to taste.

Porq Chops or Cutlets

T he Italian American term for thin cutlets is *scaloppini* (typically pork or veal). In French they are called *escalope*, and in German they are known as *schnitzel*. Prepared Porq Chops and Cutlets can be lightly dusted in seasoned flour and browned in a skillet with a small amount of cooking oil. Alternatively, they can be marinated and then pan seared in an oiled skillet or grill pan, or they can be breaded and fried. *NOTE: The prepared Porq Chops or Cutlets must be refrigerated for 8 hours prior to finishing to optimize their texture, so plan accordingly.* A marinade may be added at this time if desired.

Basic Porq Dough (page 92)
12 cups **Porq Simmering Broth** (page 93) or commercial vegetable broth

Put a stainless-steel cooling rack on a baking sheet and line the rack with parchment paper or a silicone baking mat. The cooling rack is not required, but it is recommended because it will prevent the excessive browning that would occur from direct contact with the hot baking sheet. Preheat the oven to 350 degrees F (175 degrees C).

Form the dough into chops or cutlets (see opposite page) and arrange them in a single layer on the parchment paper or baking mat. Bake uncovered on the middle oven rack for 20 minutes for cutlets or 30 minutes for chops.

Bring the broth to a boil. If the broth was made from scratch, use a slotted spoon to remove the larger solids. It's not necessary to strain the broth completely until later.

Lower the pieces into the boiling broth and immediately decrease the heat to maintain a gentle simmer. Cook uncovered for 20 minutes. Monitor the pot frequently to make sure the broth is maintained at a simmer; do not boil. Turn the pieces occasionally once they float to the top of the pot to ensure even cooking. When the chops or cutlets are done simmering, remove the pot from the heat, cover, and let them cool in the broth.

Transfer the chops or cutlets to a food storage bag (a marinade may be added at this time if desired), seal the bag, and refrigerate for 8 hours to optimize the texture before finishing. Strain the cooled broth into a sealable container and refrigerate for future use. The chops or cutlets are now ready to be finished or used in recipes as desired.

Finishing Porq Chops or Cutlets

Chops or cutlets can be seasoned as desired and browned in a nonstick skillet, grill pan, or well-seasoned cast-iron skillet. Alternatively, they can be dredged in seasoned flour or breading and fried until golden brown. Chops can be basted and pan grilled, broiled, or grilled outdoors. Brush or spray the grill pan or grill grates with cooking oil (or use a nonstick grill mat). Brushing the chops with cooking oil before grilling or broiling will help keep them moist and tender even when a sauce or glaze is being used.

How to Shape Porq Dough

CHOPS: Slice the dough with a sharp knife into 6 equal pieces. Flatten each piece with the heel of your hand to ½ inch thick. Try not to taper the edges when pressing (chops should have a sharper blocked edge as opposed to cutlets, which have a tapered edge). Use your fingers to create the characteristic "chop" shape (chops are wide at the top and narrow toward the bottom, with a gentle C-shaped curve on one side). If the dough is resistant to shaping, let it rest for a minute or two to relax the gluten.

CUTLETS: Slice the dough with a sharp knife into 8 equal pieces. Press and stretch the dough against a work surface into thin, flat cutlets. If the dough is resistant to shaping, let it rest for a minute or two to relax the gluten.

Citrus- or Balsamic-Glazed Chops

Pan-grilled porq chops are seasoned with your choice of marinade and glaze and served over fresh greens.

PORQ CHOPS

4 prepared **Porq Chops** (page 94)

2 tablespoons **cooking oil** or **nondairy butter** or **margarine**

4 cups chopped mixed **spring greens**

¼ cup chopped **fresh cilantro**, for garnish

CITRUS MARINADE AND GLAZE

¼ cup **tamari**, **soy sauce**, or **Bragg Liquid Aminos**

¼ cup fresh **lime juice**

2 tablespoons **organic sugar**

1 tablespoon **rice vinegar** or **apple cider vinegar**

2 teaspoons **grated fresh ginger** (see page 31)

1 teaspoon **sambal oelek** (Indonesian chile sauce), **sriracha sauce**, or other hot sauce

BALSAMIC MARINADE AND GLAZE

½ cup **apple juice or cider**

2 tablespoons **dark balsamic vinegar**

2 tablespoons **tamari**, **soy sauce**, or **Bragg Liquid Aminos**

2 tablespoons **raw agave syrup**

½ teaspoon **cayenne**

Prepare the chops as directed and let cool in the broth. Transfer them to a food storage bag and add all the ingredients for either the citrus marinade or the balsamic marinade. Seal the bag and refrigerate for 8 to 12 hours.

When you're ready to prepare the dish, remove the chops from the marinade, transfer to a plate, and set aside. Pour the remaining marinade into a small saucepan and bring to a simmer over medium heat. Remove from the heat and set aside.

Oil a nonstick skillet or grill pan with cooking oil or nondairy butter and place over medium heat. When the pan is hot or the butter is melted, sear the chops until golden brown on both sides. Add 2 tablespoons of the marinade while searing the chops to create a sweet-and-spicy glaze.

While the chops are browning, line individual serving plates with the greens. Top with the chops and drizzle with the warm marinade. Garnish with the cilantro and serve.

Schnitzel

German- and Austrian-inspired thin porq cutlets are breaded and fried and served with lemon slices or a sauce or gravy, such as Savory Onion Gravy (page 166). Potato salad or potatoes with parsley and butter are a traditional accompaniment.

¾ cup **all-purpose flour**

1 cup plain **nondairy milk**

1 cup fine plain dry **bread crumbs**

1½ teaspoons **sea salt** or **kosher salt**

1 teaspoon **onion powder**

1 teaspoon **paprika**

½ teaspoon **garlic powder**

½ teaspoon coarsely ground **black pepper**

4 prepared **Porq Cutlets** (page 94)

To make a batter, put the flour and milk in a small bowl and whisk until smooth. Put the bread crumbs, salt, onion powder, paprika, garlic powder, and pepper in a separate small bowl and stir to combine. Dip each cutlet in the batter and then dredge in the bread-crumb mixture, coating evenly on both sides. Transfer to a plate and let dry for 10 minutes.

Put enough cooking oil in a large skillet to reach a depth of ¼ inch and place over medium-high heat. When the oil begins to shimmer, add the cutlets and fry, turning frequently, until golden brown. Watch closely because they will brown quickly. Transfer the cutlets to a plate lined with paper towels to drain for 1 minute, then arrange on individual serving plates.

Tonkatsu

onkatsu is a Japanese dish consisting of breaded and fried porq cutlets served with a tangy sauce on the side.

KATSU SAUCE

1 teaspoon **unmodified potato starch** or **cornstarch**

½ cup **ketchup**

½ cup **water**

¼ cup **dark brown sugar**

3 tablespoons **tamari, soy sauce,** or **Bragg Liquid Aminos**

1 tablespoon **Worcestershire Sauce** (page 182) or commercial vegan equivalent

½ teaspoon **hot red pepper sauce**

¼ teaspoon **garlic powder**

BREADING

1 cup plain **nondairy milk**

¾ cup **rice flour** or **all-purpose flour**

1½ teaspoons **sea salt** or **kosher salt**

1 teaspoon **onion powder**

½ teaspoon **garlic powder**

¼ teaspoon ground **white pepper**

1 cup very fine **panko bread crumbs**, plus more if needed

PORQ CUTLETS

4 prepared **Porq Cutlets** (page 94)

Chopped **scallions**, for garnish

To make the sauce, put the starch in a small bowl or measuring cup. Add 2 teaspoons of water and stir to create a slurry. Put the ketchup, ½ cup water, brown sugar, tamari, Worcestershire Sauce, hot sauce, and garlic powder in a small saucepan and whisk to combine. Bring to a simmer over medium heat. Add the starch slurry and stir until thickened. Decrease the heat to low to keep warm until ready to serve, stirring occasionally. The sauce can also be used at room temperature.

To make the breading, put the milk, flour, salt, onion powder, garlic powder, and white pepper in a small bowl and whisk into a smooth batter. Put the bread crumbs in a separate small bowl.

Dip the cutlets first in the batter, shake off any excess, and then dredge them in the bread crumbs, making sure they are evenly coated. Transfer to a plate to dry while the oil is heated.

Put enough cooking oil in a large skillet or wok to reach a depth of ½ inch and place over medium-high heat. Test the temperature of the oil by dropping in a few bread crumbs. If the crumbs brown quickly, the oil is sufficiently hot.

Gently put the cutlets in the hot oil and fry until golden brown on each side. Transfer to a plate lined with paper towels to blot any excess oil.

Garnish a serving plate with the katsu sauce. When the cutlets are cool enough to handle, slice them and arrange the slices on the serving plate. Garnish with chopped scallions. Serve immediately with additional katsu sauce on the side.

Tips from Chef Skye ■ Very fine panko bread crumbs will adhere best to the cutlets. Crush the crumbs in a food processor to make them finer if necessary.

Pulled Porq

When porq is pulled into shreds, it amazingly resembles roasted pulled pork in flavor, aroma, and texture. It is prepared from a blend of vital wheat gluten, tofu, and select seasonings. Pulled Porq is ideal for use in recipes where a shredded texture is desired, such as Texas barbecue, Pacific Island cuisine, Mexican cuisine (burritos, carnitas, enchiladas, flautas, tamales, and taquitos), Vietnamese banh mi sandwiches, and much more! A pressure cooker is recommended for preparation; however, oven baking is an option. A food processor is required for this recipe to achieve the proper finished texture. If you have a large-capacity food processor, see page 42.

1½ cups (225 g) **vital wheat gluten**

10 ounces (284 g) extra-firm **tofu**, pressed (see page 11)

1 cup (240 ml) **water**

2 tablespoons neutral **vegetable oil**

2 tablespoons **tamari**, **soy sauce**, or **Bragg Liquid Aminos**

2 tablespoons mellow **white miso**

4 teaspoons **onion powder**

2 teaspoons **garlic powder**

1 teaspoon **mushroom powder**

1 teaspoon **hickory liquid smoke**

1 tablespoon **dry rub seasoning** (optional)

Put the vital wheat gluten in a large bowl. Set aside.

Crumble the tofu into a blender. Add the water, oil, tamari, miso, onion powder, garlic powder, mushroom powder, and liquid smoke and process until smooth and creamy. Stop the blender as necessary to scrape down the jar.

Scoop the tofu mixture into the vital wheat gluten and combine with a sturdy silicone spatula until the tofu mixture is incorporated and a sticky ball of dough begins to form. Let the dough rest for 10 minutes. This will give the gluten a chance to absorb the liquid and help reduce the stickiness.

Put the dough in a food processor fitted with a standard chopping blade or plastic dough blade and process for 2 minutes. If you have a small-capacity food processor, divide the dough in half and process each half separately to reduce wear and tear on the motor.

The processor may bounce as the dough reaches its desired elasticity. If it does, simply hold the processor in place. If the blade stops turning, turn the unit off; the dough should be sufficiently processed.

When the dough is sufficiently processed, it should be sticky, stretchy, glossy, and slightly warm. Occasionally, the sticky dough may creep up onto the motor shaft of the processor during processing. Simply clean it up with a damp paper towel.

Lay an 18-inch-long sheet of heavy-duty aluminum foil on a work surface. Transfer the dough to the foil and shape into a compact mass. If you are using a dry rub seasoning, sprinkle it evenly over the dough. Roll the dough in the foil and twist the ends tightly to seal. Bend the ends in half to lock them tight. Wrap the package in a second sheet of foil in a similar manner.

If you will be oven baking the porq (rather than pressure cooking it), twist the ends tightly but leave a small amount of air space in the package on each side to allow for expansion of the dough during baking. Wrap in a third sheet of foil for reinforcement.

To pressure cook, put 3 cups of water in the cooker and put the trivet in place. Add the package, seal the lid, close the steam valve, and cook on high for 1 hour and 30 minutes. Turn the unit off and let the steam pressure release naturally for 30 minutes. Remove the package from the cooker and let cool until it can be handled comfortably.

To oven bake (instead of pressure cook), preheat the oven to 350 degrees F (175 degrees C). Put the foil package directly on the middle oven rack and bake for 2 hours. Remove from the oven and let cool until the package can be handled comfortably.

While the roast is still warm, bend it in half lengthwise until it splits; this will reveal the "grain." Tear the roast in half following where it has been split. Bend and tear those pieces in half lengthwise. Pull the porq into long shreds, following the grain as much as possible. Tear those pieces into smaller bite-sized shreds, once again following the grain as much as possible. Use in recipes as desired. Store in an airtight container in the refrigerator and use within 1 week.

Tips from Chef Skye

- For additional flavor, use a dry seasoning rub prior to wrapping and cooking the porq.
- For soups and stews, Pulled Porq should be added 20 minutes before serving to retain the optimum texture.
- See the troubleshooting tips on page 46.

Barbecue and Teriyaki Pulled Porq

Barbecue Pulled Porq makes superb Texas-style sandwiches served on soft buns or rolls. Teriyaki Pulled Porq is splendid served over steamed rice.

2 tablespoons **cooking oil**

1 medium **onion**, thinly sliced

½ **green bell pepper**, thinly sliced

3 cloves **garlic**, minced (1 tablespoon)

12 ounces prepared **Pulled Porq** (page 102), in bite-sized shreds

½ cup **barbecue sauce** or **teriyaki sauce**, plus more as desired

Coarsely ground **black pepper**

Put the oil in a large nonstick skillet or wok over medium heat. When the oil is hot, add the onion and bell pepper and sauté until tender. Add the garlic and sauté for 30 seconds.

Add the Pulled Porq and sauté, tossing frequently, until lightly browned. Add the barbecue or teriyaki sauce and toss well until evenly distributed. Cook until heated through. Season with pepper to taste.

Cuban-Style Pulled Porq

ender shreds of porq are sautéed in fresh citrus juices with onion and an abundance of garlic to create this popular Cuban-style dish. Serve it with rice and beans and soft flour tortillas.

¼ cup freshly squeezed **orange juice**

2 tablespoons freshly squeezed **lime juice**

2 tablespoons **cooking oil**

1 large **onion**, halved and thinly sliced

9 cloves **garlic**, minced

1 tablespoon minced **fresh oregano**, or 1 teaspoon dried oregano

½ teaspoon **fresh orange zest**

½ teaspoon **fresh lime zest**

1½ pounds prepared **Pulled Porq** (page 102), in bite-sized shreds

Sea salt or **kosher salt**

Coarsely ground **black pepper**

Lime wedges, for garnish

Put the orange juice and lime juice in a small bowl and stir to combine. Set aside.

Put the oil in a large nonstick skillet or wok over medium heat. Add the onion and sauté until tender and translucent. Add the garlic, oregano, orange zest, and lime zest and sauté for 30 seconds.

Add the porq and sauté, tossing frequently, until lightly browned. Drizzle in the reserved citrus juice mixture and toss well until evenly distributed. Continue to sauté until almost all the liquid has evaporated but the porq is still moist. Season with salt and pepper to taste. Transfer to a serving platter and garnish with lime wedges.

Carnitas (MEXICAN-STYLE PULLED PORQ)

Tender shreds of porq are sautéed with onion, green chiles, garlic, lime juice, and south-of-the-border seasonings for this classic Mexican dish. Serve it with warm tortillas and fresh guacamole on the side.

1 teaspoon **ground cumin**

1 teaspoon **ground coriander**

1 teaspoon **dried oregano**

1 teaspoon **dried marjoram**

2 tablespoons **cooking oil**

1 large **onion**, halved and thinly sliced

1 large **jalapeño or serrano chile**, seeded and minced

6 cloves **garlic**, minced (2 tablespoons)

1½ pounds prepared **Pulled Porq** (page 102), in bite-sized shreds

¼ cup freshly squeezed **lime juice**

Sea salt or **kosher salt**

Coarsely ground **black pepper**

Chopped **fresh cilantro**, for garnish

Put the cumin, coriander, oregano, and marjoram in a small dish and stir to combine. Set aside.

Put the oil in a large nonstick skillet or wok over medium heat. Add the onion and chile and sauté until tender. Add the garlic and sauté for 30 seconds. Add the porq and sauté, tossing frequently, until lightly browned. Add the lime juice and reserved seasonings and toss well until evenly distributed.

Continue to sauté until almost all the liquid has evaporated but the porq is still moist. Season with salt and pepper to taste. Garnish generously with chopped cilantro.

Polynesian Pulled Porq

Tender shreds of smoky, salty porq are sautéed with onion, garlic, and ginger for this Polynesian-style favorite. Serve it with sticky rice and other island side dishes, such as macaroni salad, to create the famous Hawaiian plate lunch.

2 tablespoons **water**

1 tablespoon **hickory liquid smoke**, plus more if desired

1 teaspoon **Hawaiian red alae salt**, **coarse sea salt**, or **kosher salt**,
    plus more as needed

2 tablespoons **cooking oil**

1 large **sweet yellow or Maui onion**, halved and very thinly sliced

6 cloves **garlic**, minced (2 tablespoons)

2 teaspoons grated **fresh ginger** (see page 31)

1½ pounds prepared **Pulled Porq** (page 102), in bite-sized shreds

Chopped **scallions**, for garnish

Put the water, liquid smoke, and salt in a small dish and stir until the salt dissolves. Set aside.

Put the oil in a large nonstick skillet or wok over medium heat. Add the onion and sauté until tender and translucent. Add the garlic and ginger and sauté for 30 seconds.

Add the porq and sauté, tossing frequently, until lightly browned. Add the reserved liquid smoke mixture and toss well until evenly distributed.

Continue to sauté until almost all the liquid has evaporated but the porq is still moist. Season with additional salt to taste (Polynesian porq should be a bit salty). Garnish with chopped scallions.

Chili Verde

T ender white beans and shreds of porq are simmered in a zesty sauce made with tomatillos and green chiles, then topped with chopped cilantro, nondairy sour cream, and shredded vegan cheese. Serve it with warm flour tortillas.

1 can (28 ounces) **tomatillos**, drained

1 cup commercial **vegetable broth**

2 tablespoons **olive oil**

1 large **onion**, diced

2 large **jalapeño or serrano chiles**, seeded and finely diced

5 cloves **garlic**, minced

2 cans (4 ounces each) diced **mild green chiles**, drained

1 can (15 ounces) **white beans**, such as cannellini, navy, or great Northern, drained and rinsed

1 teaspoon **dried oregano**

½ teaspoon **ground cumin**

½ teaspoon **ground coriander**

½ teaspoon coarsely ground **black pepper**

12 ounces prepared **Pulled Porq** (page 102), in bite-sized shreds

Sea salt or **kosher salt**

Shredded **vegan cheese**, for garnish

Nondairy **sour cream**, for garnish

Chopped **cilantro**, for garnish

Put the tomatillos and broth in a blender and pulse a few times to coarsely chop the tomatillos (they should retain some texture). Pour into a large pot and place over low heat.

Put the oil in a medium skillet over medium heat. Add the onion and fresh chiles and sauté until the onion is translucent. Add the garlic and sauté until the onion is just beginning to lightly brown. Transfer to the pot with the tomatillos.

Add the canned chiles, white beans, oregano, cumin, coriander, and pepper to the pot. Increase the heat to medium and bring to a simmer. Decrease the heat to medium-low, partially cover, and cook, stirring occasionally, for 30 minutes.

Stir in the porq and simmer for 5 minutes. Season with salt to taste. Ladle the chili into individual serving bowls and top with shredded cheese, sour cream, and cilantro as desired.

Country-Style Ribz and Rack Ribz

C ountry-Style Ribz ("boneless") and Rack Ribz ("bone-in") are particularly well suited for outdoor grilling or any time you're using a grill pan or broiler. Although the Rack Ribz require a little more work, they're fun to make, and barbecued ribz are always better when you have something to grasp while eating. This recipe creates ribz that are chewy on the outside and moist and tender on the inside, with a wonderful pull-apart texture. The secret to the texture is the tofu and shredded onion.

1 cup (150 g) **vital wheat gluten**

1 medium **onion**

2½ ounces (70 g) extra-firm block **tofu**, pressed (see page 11)

½ cup (120 ml) **water**

1 tablespoon neutral **vegetable oil**

1 tablespoon **tamari, soy sauce**, or **Bragg Liquid Aminos**

1 tablespoon mellow **white miso**

2 teaspoons **onion powder**

2 teaspoons **garlic powder**

1 teaspoon **mushroom powder**

Grilling sauce or glaze

Preheat the oven to 350 degrees F (175 degrees C). Put the vital wheat gluten in a large bowl and set aside.

Shred the onion on the largest holes of a box grater. The shredded onion will be very wet. Shred enough of the onion to pack ¼ cup, including liquid. Set aside.

Crumble the tofu into a blender. Add the water, oil, tamari, miso, onion powder, garlic powder, and mushroom powder and process until smooth and creamy. Stop the blender as necessary to scrape down the jar.

Scoop the tofu mixture into the vital wheat gluten, add the shredded onion, and combine with a sturdy silicone spatula until the tofu and onion are incorporated and a ball of dough begins to form. Knead the dough in the bowl until it begins to exhibit some elasticity, about 2 minutes.

Shape the dough to make Country-Style Ribz or Rack Ribz (see page 111). Bake on the middle oven rack for 45 minutes. Remove the pan (with the foil in place) or package from the oven to cool. Refrigerate the pan or package for 8 hours to optimize the texture of the ribz before finishing.

To finish Country-Style Ribz, flip the contents of the pan onto a work surface. Cut the slab in half down the center. With a knife, lightly score one segment to create 6 ribz. Avoid cutting all the way through. Repeat with the remaining segment. To finish Rack Ribz, cut the rack down the center to create 2 segments. Now the ribz are ready for grilling or broiling.

To pan grill the ribz, oil a nonstick grill pan. For outdoor grilling, brush or spray the grill grates with cooking oil or use a nonstick grill mat. Brush the ribz with cooking oil. Grill the ribz until lightly browned on each side. Brush generously with grilling sauce or glaze and continue to grill, turning occasionally, until the sauce begins to caramelize.

To broil the ribz (instead of pan grill), set the oven to "broil." Line a baking sheet with foil or parchment paper and arrange the ribz on it in a single layer. Brush the ribz with cooking oil and then broil until they are lightly browned,

about 3 minutes on each side. Watch carefully so the ribz don't burn. Brush generously with the sauce and continue to broil, turning occasionally, until the sauce begins to caramelize.

Transfer to a serving platter. Serve with additional sauce on the side if desired. Pull the individual ribz apart to eat.

How to Shape Ribz

COUNTRY-STYLE RIBZ: Line an 8-inch square baking pan with parchment paper or aluminum foil.

Pick up the dough, stretch it (as if you were stretching pizza dough), and put it in the baking pan. Press, stretch, and flatten the dough to completely fill the bottom of the pan.

Cover the pan with a sheet of foil and press the foil into the pan, covering the surface of the dough. Seal the foil around the edges of the pan. The foil needs to be in contact with the surface of the dough to seal in moisture. If you want to prevent the foil from coming in contact with the ribz, cover the ribz with a sheet of parchment paper cut to fit the inside of the pan and then cover with the foil as directed.

RACK RIBZ: For this technique, you will need 12 wooden craft sticks (ice-cream sticks). With a knife, cut the dough into 4 equal pieces, then cut each quarter into 3 equal pieces for a total of 12 pieces.

Lay a 24-inch-long sheet of heavy-duty aluminum foil horizontally on a work surface.

Pick up a piece of dough, roll it between the palms of your hands to create a short "rope," and then gently stretch it as far as you can. If it tears too easily, knead the dough until it can be stretched.

Wrap a piece of the dough around one of the sticks, leaving ½ inch of the stick free for grasping. Pinch both ends of the dough to prevent it from unwinding. If the dough tears, simply press it together at the breaking point and continue. Perfection is not required. Place the individual "rib" on the foil. Repeat with the remaining dough and sticks, placing each rib next to the last one, and lining them up so they are touching each other.

With the palms of your hands, firmly flatten the ribz until they are about ½ inch thick while simultaneously pushing them together. This will create a connection point so the ribz can adhere to each other. As they bake, the ribz will expand and the adhesion will be complete. This only needs to be done on one side; it's not necessary to flip the ribz over. Fold the ribz in the foil to create a flattened package. Fold in the ends and crimp to seal shut.

Sweet-and-Smoky Bacun

YIELDS 1½ POUNDS

S weet-and-Smoky Bacun is prepared with vital wheat gluten, tofu, and a select blend of seasonings. This combination produces a finished product that is remarkably similar to real bacon in appearance, texture, and flavor, with a nice balance of salty, smoky, and sweet. Chop, dice, or crumble the bacun in recipes. It also makes a fantastic filling for a BLT sandwich.

There are several steps to this recipe, but don't be intimidated because it's relatively easy to prepare, and the results are well worth the effort. Two batches of dough will be mixed to create the bacun. Dough 1 is for the light marble layer and Dough 2 is for the dark marble layer. A pressure cooker is recommended for preparation; however, oven baking is an option. A food processor is required for this recipe to achieve the proper finished texture.

DOUGH 1

5 ounces (142 g) extra-firm **tofu**, pressed (see page 11)

1 tablespoon **olive oil**

2 teaspoons **garlic powder**

1 teaspoon **sea salt** or **kosher salt**

½ cup **water**

½ cup **vital wheat gluten**

DOUGH 2

5 ounces (142 g) extra-firm **tofu**, pressed (see page 11)

6 tablespoons **tamari**, **soy sauce**, or **Bragg Liquid Aminos**

1 tablespoon **hickory liquid smoke**

1 tablespoon **light brown sugar**

1 tablespoon **Worcestershire Sauce** (page 182) or commercial vegan equivalent

4 teaspoons **onion powder**

1 tablespoon **olive oil**

1 tablespoon **smoked paprika**

1 cup **vital wheat gluten**

¼ cup **water**

OPTIONAL RUB

1 teaspoon smoked **black pepper** or coarsely ground black pepper

Real maple syrup or **brown sugar** (optional; for sweeter bacun)

To prepare Dough 1, crumble the tofu into a food processor. Add the oil, garlic powder, salt, and 2 tablespoons of the water. Process until as smooth as possible, stopping to scrape down the sides of the work bowl as needed. Add the vital wheat gluten and the remaining water and process for 1 minute. Divide the dough into 2 equal pieces and set aside. There's no need to rinse or wash the work bowl.

To prepare Dough 2, crumble the tofu into the food processor. Add the tamari, liquid smoke, brown sugar, Worcestershire Sauce, onion powder, oil, and smoked paprika. Process until as smooth as possible, stopping to scrape down the sides of the work bowl as needed. Add the vital wheat gluten and water and process for 2 minutes. Divide the dough into 3 equal pieces and set aside.

Lay an 18-inch-long sheet of heavy-duty aluminum foil on a work surface. Take a piece of Dough 2, flatten it into a disk, and place it on the foil. Repeat the process with a piece of Dough 1 and place it on top of the first disk. Repeat with the remaining pieces of dough, alternating them as you stack.

Firmly press down on the stack until it is about 1 inch thick. Press and shape the dough into a compact, square slab. Don't worry about being too precise, as the dough will expand during baking to conform to the shape of the foil package.

If desired, season the surface of the dough with ½ teaspoon of the optional black pepper. Flip the slab over and repeat with the remaining pepper. For "candied" bacun, rub the exterior of the dough with maple syrup or pack with brown sugar.

To wrap the dough, fold (don't roll) the foil over the slab of bacun several times to create a flat package. Fold in the sides and crimp to seal the package. Wrap it in a second sheet of foil in the same manner.

If you will be oven baking the dough, leave some air space on each side of the package as the sides are folded in and crimped to allow for expansion of the dough as it bakes. Wrap it in a third sheet of foil for reinforcement.

To pressure cook, put 3 cups of water in the cooker and put the trivet in place. Add the package, seal the lid, close the steam valve, and cook on high for 1 hour and 45 minutes. Turn the cooker off and let the pressure release naturally for 30 minutes. Remove the package from the cooker and let cool for 1 hour.

To oven bake (instead of pressure cook), preheat the oven to 350 degrees F (175 degrees C). Put the package directly on the middle oven rack and bake for 2 hours. Remove from the oven and let cool for 1 hour.

To finish, refrigerate the package for 8 hours to optimize the bacun's texture before slicing. For the best finished texture, use an electric slicer or a very sharp knife and slice the bacun as thinly as possible (unless you prefer a thicker cut). When sliced thin, the bacun may tatter a bit, but this only adds to the authentic finished texture and appearance.

To oven brown the bacun, preheat the oven to 375 degrees F (190 degrees C). Line a baking sheet with aluminum foil or parchment paper and arrange the slices on it in a single layer. Generously brush the slices on both sides with cooking oil. Bake for 15 to 20 minutes. Transfer to a plate lined with paper towels to blot any excess oil.

To fry the bacun, put a generous layer of cooking oil in a large skillet over medium heat (to prevent burning, avoid frying it at a high temperature). Cook until lightly browned on both sides. Transfer to a plate lined with paper towels to blot any excess oil.

As the bacun cools, it will crisp up a bit while still retaining a chewy texture.

Tips from Chef Skye ■ It's helpful to put a heavy object, such as a cast-iron skillet, on the foil package to compress it as it cools and keep the slab of bacun flat. This will also help to compress the bacun and improve its texture.

Garden Ham

Generously flavored with hickory smoke, brown sugar, and warm spices, Garden Ham is reminiscent of a natural uncured ham and can be served hot or cold. For deli-style shaved ham, use an electric deli slicer for uniform thin slices; thick slices are ideal for pan grilling. The ham can be cooked in an oven or pressure cooker; however, an oven will be needed for glazing and reheating the ham (see page 117). Spicy brown or Dijon mustard is the ideal condiment for enhancing the flavor of the sliced ham.

AROMATIC BRINE

2¼ cups (540 ml) **water**

2 tablespoons **nutritional yeast flakes**

2 tablespoons **light brown sugar**

2 tablespoons **red miso**, or 1 tablespoon **tamari** and 1 tablespoon **tomato paste**

2 tablespoons **hickory liquid smoke**

2 tablespoons neutral **vegetable oil**

2¼ teaspoons **sea salt** or **kosher salt**

2 teaspoons whole **cloves**, plus more if a stronger clove flavor is desired

½ teaspoon **ground ginger**

½ teaspoon **ground white pepper**

DRY INGREDIENTS

2 cups (300 g) **vital wheat gluten**

¼ cup **all-purpose flour**

2 tablespoons **onion powder**

1 tablespoon **garlic powder**

To make the brine, put the water in a medium saucepan. Bring to a boil over medium-high heat, then remove from the heat. Add the remaining brine ingredients and stir until the nutritional yeast, brown sugar, miso, and salt dissolve. Let cool to near room temperature (the mixture must cool before proceeding; do not add hot brine to the dry ingredients!)

To make the ham dough, put all the dry ingredients in a large bowl and whisk to combine. Strain the cooled brine through a fine sieve into the dry ingredients and discard the strained solids (straining will remove any whole and undissolved seasoning sediment). Combine thoroughly with a sturdy silicone spatula to develop the gluten. Let the dough rest for 10 minutes to allow the dry ingredients to absorb as much liquid as possible.

To wrap the dough, lay an 18-inch-long sheet of heavy-duty aluminum foil on a work surface. Put the dough directly on the foil and form it into a round mass. The dough will be soft and will tend to spread out; try to keep it as compact as you can.

Lift an edge of the foil over the dough and begin rolling it into a cylinder while simultaneously pinching the ends closed. The goal is to create a thick, compact, cylindrical package. This may take practice, so be patient. Twist the ends tightly to seal, taking care to not tear the foil. Bend the twisted ends in half to lock them tight.

Wrap with a second sheet of foil in a similar manner. If you will be oven baking the dough (rather than pressure cooking it), wrap it in a third sheet of foil for reinforcement.

To pressure cook, put 3 cups of water in the cooker and put the trivet in place. Add the package, seal the lid, close the steam valve, and cook on high for 1 hour and 45 minutes. Turn the unit off and let the pressure release naturally for 30 minutes. Remove the package and let cool.

To oven bake (instead of pressure cook), preheat the oven to 350 degrees F (175 degrees C). Put the foil package directly on the middle oven rack and bake for 2 hours. Remove the package and let cool.

Refrigerate the ham in the foil wrapper for 8 hours to optimize the texture and make cold slicing easier. Serve hot, cold, or at room temperature.

Glazed Ham

arden Ham can be finished with savory Tamari-Pepper Glaze or sweet-and-spicy Brown Sugar and Mustard Glaze, but you can also use any sweet, spicy, or savory glaze of your choice. It's not necessary to refrigerate the ham after pressure cooking or oven baking; you can simply glaze the ham immediately afterward. However, if the ham was refrigerated, let the package come to room temperature for 1 hour before glazing it.

TAMARI-PEPPER GLAZE

2 tablespoons **nondairy butter** or **margarine**

2 tablespoons **tamari, soy sauce,** or **Bragg Liquid Aminos**

Coarsely ground smoked or regular **black pepper**

Preheat the oven to 350 degrees F (175 degrees C). Put the butter in a large skillet over medium heat until melted. Add the whole ham and lightly brown it all over. Add the tamari and continue to glaze the ham until it is evenly browned. Season with black pepper to taste. Transfer to a baking dish, cover with foil, and bake for 30 minutes. Transfer to a cutting board or serving platter for slicing.

BROWN SUGAR AND MUSTARD GLAZE

2 tablespoons dark **brown sugar**

1 tablespoon **Dijon** or **spicy mustard**

1 teaspoon **tamari, soy sauce,** or **Bragg Liquid Aminos**

1 teaspoon **hickory liquid smoke**

2 tablespoons **nondairy butter** or **margarine**

Preheat the oven to 350 degrees F (175 degrees C). Put the brown sugar, mustard, tamari, and liquid smoke in a small dish and stir until the sugar dissolves. Set aside.

Put the butter in a large skillet over medium heat until melted. Add the whole ham and lightly brown it all over. Transfer to a baking dish and brush with the glaze until evenly coated. Cover with foil and bake for 30 minutes. Transfer to a cutting board or serving platter for slicing.

Split Pea Soup with Garden Ham

Tender split peas, onion, carrots, and potatoes merge to create this classic soup. The ham adds a wonderful smoky flavor. *NOTE: The dried split peas need to be soaked for 2 hours prior to cooking, so plan accordingly.*

10 ounces **dried split green peas** (about 1¼ cups by volume)

2 tablespoons **olive oil**

1 large **onion**, diced

2 large **carrots**, peeled and diced

3 cloves **garlic**, minced

8 cups **Porq Simmering Broth** (page 93) or commercial vegetable broth

2 **russet potatoes**, peeled and diced

½ teaspoon **dried thyme**

¼ teaspoon coarsely ground **black pepper**, plus more as needed

1½ cups diced **Garden Ham** (page 115)

Sea salt or **kosher salt**

Put the split peas in a roomy heatproof container (such as a mason jar) and add boiling water to cover. Let soak for 2 hours. Drain well and set aside.

Put the oil in a large pot over medium heat. Add the onion and carrots and sauté until the onion is translucent. Add the garlic and sauté for 1 minute. Add the broth, potatoes, split peas, thyme, and pepper. Bring to a boil, then decrease the heat to maintain a gentle simmer. Cover the pot and cook for 1 hour and 30 minutes. Stir occasionally to prevent the solids from scorching and sticking to the bottom of the pot.

Add the ham the last 10 minutes of cooking. Season the soup with salt and additional pepper to taste.

House Specials

Holiday Roast Turky

Holiday Roast Turky is created from a blend of vital wheat gluten, tofu, and select seasonings. The roast is partially baked and then simmered in a special broth to complete the preparation process. After simmering, the remaining broth can be used for sauces, gravies, soups, or stews. The roast is finished by first being wrapped in rice paper to create a "skin." Then it's pan-glazed until golden brown and crispy and reheated in the oven before being sliced and served. A food processor fitted with a plastic dough blade or standard chopping blade is recommended but not required for this recipe. If you have a large-capacity food processor, see page 42. *NOTE: The prepared Roast Turky must be refrigerated for 8 hours prior to finishing to optimize its texture, so plan accordingly.*

2 cups (300 g) **vital wheat gluten**

¼ cup **all-purpose flour**

10 ounces (284 g) extra-firm **tofu**, pressed (see page 11)

1½ cups (360 ml) **water**

2 tablespoons neutral **vegetable oil**

2 tablespoons mellow **white miso**

4 teaspoons **onion powder**

2 teaspoons **garlic powder**

2 teaspoons **sea salt** or **kosher salt**

1 teaspoon **poultry seasoning** or **Aromatica** (page 161)

16 cups **Turky Simmering Broth** (page 123)

3 sheets **rice paper** (spring roll wrappers), or fresh **yuba** (tofu skin)

3 tablespoons **nondairy butter** or **margarine**

1 tablespoon **tamari**, **soy sauce**, or **Bragg Liquid Aminos**

2 tablespoons **dry white wine** or **Turky Simmering Broth** (page 123)

1 teaspoon minced **fresh rosemary** (optional)

1 teaspoon minced **fresh sage** (optional)

1 teaspoon minced **fresh thyme** (optional)

Coarsely ground **black pepper**

Put the vital wheat gluten and flour in a large bowl and stir with a whisk to combine. Set aside.

Crumble the tofu into a blender. Add the water, oil, miso, onion powder, garlic powder, salt, and poultry seasoning and process until smooth and creamy. Stop the blender as necessary to scrape down the jar.

Scoop the tofu mixture into the vital wheat gluten mixture and combine with a sturdy silicone spatula until the tofu mixture is incorporated and a ball of dough begins to form. The mixture may seem a bit dry at first. Do not add more water.

Transfer the dough to a work surface and knead vigorously for 3 to 4 minutes. This is important in order to develop the gluten. Test the dough by stretching it. If it tears easily, more kneading is required. Alternatively, put the dough in a stand mixer fitted with a dough hook and process on low speed for 1 minute.

Preheat the oven to 350 degrees F (175 degrees C).

Lay a 24-inch-long sheet of aluminum foil on a work surface (if you prefer, use 2 large sheets of parchment paper). Transfer the dough to the foil and shape into a compact oval. Roll the dough in the foil and then fold the ends under to create a package. Do not seal the package. The foil (or parchment) is being used only to hold the shape of the roast, not wrap it air tight. Put the package on a baking sheet and bake on the middle oven rack for 1 hour.

Unwrap and pierce the roast 4 times on the top and 4 times on the bottom with a fork. The roast will be very soft at this stage, so handle carefully.

Bring the broth to a boil. Carefully lower the roast into the broth. Decrease the heat to maintain a simmer, partially cover, and cook for 1 hour. Turn the roast occasionally as it simmers.

Monitor the pot frequently and adjust the heat as necessary to maintain a simmer. The broth should be gently bubbling. Do not boil, but do not let the roast merely poach in the hot broth either, as a gentle simmer is necessary to penetrate the roast and finish the cooking process.

Remove the pot from the heat, cover, and let the roast cool in the broth. Transfer the cooled roast to a food storage bag, seal the bag, and refrigerate for 8 hours to optimize the texture. Strain the cooled broth into a sealable container and refrigerate for future use.

To finish the roast, bring it to room temperature for 1 hour before finishing. Preheat the oven to 350 degrees F (175 degrees C).

Put the roast on a work surface. Soak the rice paper briefly in warm water to soften. Drape over the roast, forming it over the top and tucking the ends under the bottom. The rice paper will continue to soften and become more flexible within a few minutes. The goal is to completely seal the roast with the rice paper. Stretch the softened, elastic paper as needed to achieve this goal. Alternatively, the roast can be wrapped in yuba (tofu skin) in a similar manner. (Yuba does not need to be soaked before using.)

Put the butter in a large, deep nonstick skillet or wok over medium heat until melted. Add the roast and cook, turning occasionally, until it is golden all over.

Add the tamari and continue to cook and turn the roast for about 1 minute. Add the wine or broth, optional herbs (rosemary, sage, and thyme), and a few pinches of black pepper. Continue to pan-glaze until the liquid has evaporated and the roast achieves a rich brown color. Be sure to run a stove exhaust fan while pan-glazing, as some smoke will be produced.

Transfer to a shallow baking dish, cover with foil, and bake for 30 minutes to heat through.

Transfer the roast to a serving platter, slice, and serve immediately.

Tips from Chef Skye
- Spooning hot broth over the sliced roast will keep the slices moist on the serving platter.
- Thinly sliced leftover roast makes superb hot or cold sandwiches. For hot sandwiches, slice the cold roast and then wrap the slices securely in foil. Put the foil package in a hot oven or in a steamer until heated through. Serve with Amber Waves of Gravy (page 170).

Turky Simmering Broth

Turky Simmering Broth is used for simmering the dough for Holiday Roast Turky (page 120) as part of the preparation process. It can also be used as a base for soups, stews, and golden-colored sauces and gravies.

16 cups (4 quarts) **water**

4 large **onions**, peeled and quartered

4 ribs **celery**, chopped

2 **carrots**, unpeeled and chopped

⅓ cup **nutritional yeast flakes**

8 cloves **garlic**, crushed

2 tablespoons **tamari**, **soy sauce**, or **Bragg Liquid Aminos**

6 sprigs **fresh thyme**, or 2 teaspoons **dried thyme**

2 tablespoons chopped **fresh sage**, or 2 teaspoons **dried rubbed sage**

4 teaspoons **sea salt** or **kosher salt**

1 sprig **fresh rosemary**, or 2 teaspoons **dried rosemary**

2 **bay leaves**

2 teaspoons **organic sugar**

1½ teaspoons **whole black peppercorns**

Small handful **parsley stems**

Put all the ingredients in a large pot, cover, and simmer over medium-low heat for 1 hour. Season with additional salt to taste. Remove the larger solids with a slotted spoon before adding the turky.

After simmering the turky, let the broth cool, then strain it into a sealable container to remove any remaining solids, and refrigerate. During this time, any sediment from the seasonings will settle on the bottom of the container.

The broth can be refrigerated for 1 week or frozen for up to 3 months. To use, decant the clear portion and discard the fine sediment. Be sure to add back water as necessary before using, since the broth will have become concentrated from evaporation during simmering.

If you're using the broth immediately for other purposes, strain it through a fine sieve into a clean pot and discard the solids.

Greek Gyros Roast

T ender slices of roast seitan are generously seasoned with aromatic Mediterranean herbs and spices. Serve warm, thin slices of the roast in a pita pocket along with sliced onion, chopped tomatoes, and Greek Tzatziki Sauce (page 175) to create the classic Greek gyros (pronounced *yee-row*) sandwich. Döner is the name of the Turkish variant of this roast. A pressure cooker is recommended for preparation; however, oven baking is an option.

1½ cups (225 g) **vital wheat gluten**

2 tablespoons **mushroom powder**

1 tablespoon **dried minced onion**

1 tablespoon **onion powder**

½ teaspoon coarsely ground **black pepper**

1½ cups (360 ml) **water**

3 tablespoons **tamari**, **soy sauce**, or **Bragg Liquid Aminos**

2 tablespoons **olive oil**

2 teaspoons **ground cumin**

2 teaspoons **dried marjoram**

1 teaspoon **dried oregano**

½ teaspoon **ground rosemary**

½ teaspoon **browning liquid** (color enhancer; optional)

4 cloves **garlic**, minced

Put the vital wheat gluten, mushroom powder, dried onion, onion powder, and pepper in a large bowl and stir to combine.

Put the water, tamari, oil, cumin, marjoram, oregano, rosemary, and optional browning liquid in a blender and process until smooth. Pour into the vital wheat gluten mixture, add the garlic, and combine thoroughly with a sturdy silicone spatula to develop the gluten. Let the dough rest for 10 minutes to allow the dry ingredients to absorb as much liquid as possible.

Lay an 18-inch-long sheet of heavy-duty aluminum foil on a work surface. Place the dough directly on top and form it into a round mass. The dough will be soft and have a tendency to spread out, but try to keep it as compact as you can. Lift the edge of the foil over the dough and begin rolling it into a cylinder while simultaneously pinching the ends closed. The goal is to create a thick, compact, cylindrical package. Due to the softness of the dough, this may take practice, so be patient. Twist the ends tightly to seal. Bend the twisted ends in half to lock them tight. Wrap in a second sheet of foil in the same manner. If you will be oven baking the dough (rather than pressure cooking it), wrap it in a third sheet of foil for reinforcement.

To pressure cook, put 3 cups of water in the cooker and put the trivet in place. Add the package, seal the lid, close the steam valve, and cook on high for 1 hour and 30 minutes. Turn the unit off and let the pressure release naturally for 30 minutes. Remove the package from the cooker and let cool for 1 hour.

To oven bake (instead of pressure cook), preheat the oven to 350 degrees F (175 degrees C). Put the package directly on the middle oven rack and bake for 1 hour and 45 minutes. Remove from the oven and let cool for 1 hour.

Refrigerate the package for 8 hours to optimize the texture and make thin slicing easier.

To finish the roast, stand it upright and shave thin slices with a sharp knife. Pan sear the slices in a lightly oiled nonstick skillet or well-seasoned cast-iron skillet until lightly browned.

New-Fashioned Meatloaf

This recipe was created after many trials and disappointments with other plant-based meatloaf recipes. It's firm yet tender and moist, with a nice balance of seasonings. Leftovers make superb meatloaf sandwiches.

LIQUID INGREDIENTS

2 cups (480 ml) **water**

3 tablespoons **tamari**, **soy sauce**, or **Bragg Liquid Aminos**

2 teaspoons **Worcestershire Sauce** (page 182) or commercial vegan equivalent

1 tablespoon **ketchup**

1 teaspoon **browning liquid** (color enhancer)

1 teaspoon **Dijon, yellow, or golden mustard**

DRY INGREDIENTS

¾ cup (113 g) **vital wheat gluten**

¼ cup **garbanzo bean flour**

2 teaspoons **onion powder**

2 teaspoons **mushroom powder**

1 teaspoon **garlic powder**

1 teaspoon **dried oregano**

½ teaspoon **dried thyme**

½ teaspoon coarsely ground **black pepper**

PROTEIN MIX AND GLAZE

2 tablespoons **olive oil**

½ cup finely diced **onion**

1 large **jalapeño or serrano chile**, seeded and finely diced, or ¼ cup finely diced **red or green bell pepper**

2 large cloves **garlic**, minced

1½ cups **textured vegetable/soy protein granules**

½ cup chopped **fresh parsley**, lightly packed

3 tablespoons **ketchup**

1 tablespoon **Dijon, golden, or yellow mustard**

1 teaspoon **Worcestershire Sauce** (page 182) or commercial vegan equivalent

Line a 9 x 5-inch standard metal loaf pan with parchment paper, leaving the excess hanging over the sides. The excess will be used to cover the meatloaf before baking and will aid the removal of the meatloaf from the pan after baking. Set aside.

Put the liquid ingredients in a large bowl and stir to combine. (Don't worry about dispersing the mustard completely; it will take care of itself later.) Set aside.

Put the dry ingredients in a large bowl and whisk to combine. Set aside.

To prepare the protein mix, put the oil in a large skillet over medium heat. Add the onion and chile and sauté until the onion is translucent. Add the garlic and sauté just until the vegetables are lightly browned around the edges. Add the liquid ingredients and bring to a boil.

Add the protein granules to the boiling liquid and stir well until evenly moistened. Stir in the parsley, cover, and remove from the heat. Let rest for 30 minutes.

Preheat the oven to 350 degrees F (175 degrees C).

Scoop the skillet ingredients into the dry ingredients, including any liquid, and fold the contents with a sturdy silicone spatula until the dry ingredients are thoroughly and evenly combined with the wet mixture. This is important, as the vital wheat gluten needs to be evenly distributed in order for the meatloaf to hold together when sliced.

Transfer the mixture to the loaf pan, firmly packing it into the pan while smoothing out the surface. Fold the excess parchment paper over the loaf and then seal the loaf pan securely with foil. Bake on the middle oven rack for 1 hour.

Make the glaze while the meatloaf is baking. Put the ketchup, mustard, and Worcestershire Sauce in a small bowl and stir until well combined. Set aside.

When the meatloaf has baked for 1 hour, remove it from the oven (but keep the oven on), remove the foil, and fold back the parchment. Evenly spread the glaze mixture over the top. Return meatloaf to the oven and bake uncovered for 15 minutes.

Remove from the oven and let cool for 15 minutes before lifting the meatloaf from the pan and transferring it to a work surface for slicing.

Tips from Chef Skye ▪ To reheat leftovers, wrap securely in foil. Preheat the oven to 350 degrees F (175 degrees C) and bake for 20 minutes.

Grillin' Burgers

At last! Homemade plant-based burgers with the appearance, flavor, and texture of real ground-beef burgers. The best part is they're 100 percent cruelty-free! Serve them on plates or buns along with your favorite condiments. A 4-inch ring mold is helpful for shaping the burgers but not essential.

WET INGREDIENTS

2 tablespoons **textured vegetable/soy protein granules**

2 tablespoons boiling **water**

¾ cup (180 ml) **water**

2 tablespoons **tamari, soy sauce, or Bragg Liquid Aminos**

2 teaspoons **Worcestershire Sauce** (page 182) or commercial vegan equivalent

1 tablespoon **olive oil**

½ teaspoon **browning liquid** (color enhancer)

DRY INGREDIENTS

1 cup (150 g) **vital wheat gluten**

1 tablespoon **garbanzo bean flour**

1 tablespoon **dried minced onion**

2 teaspoons **onion powder**

2 teaspoons **mushroom powder**

1½ teaspoons **garlic powder**

½ teaspoon coarsely ground **black pepper**

¼ teaspoon **ground rosemary**

FINISHING MARINADE

¼ cup **water**

2 teaspoons **hickory liquid smoke**

1 teaspoon **Worcestershire Sauce** (page 182) or commercial vegan equivalent

Put the protein granules in a small bowl. Add the boiling water and let the granules rehydrate for 10 minutes.

Put the remaining wet ingredients in a separate small bowl. Add the rehydrated granules and stir to combine.

Preheat the oven to 350 degrees F (175 degrees C). Put a stainless-steel cooling rack on a baking sheet and line the rack with parchment paper or a silicone baking mat. The cooling rack is not required but is recommended, as it will prevent excessive browning that would occur from direct contact with the hot baking sheet.

Put the dry ingredients in a large bowl and whisk until well combined. Give the wet ingredients a quick stir and then pour all at once into the dry ingredients. Fold the mixture together with a sturdy silicone spatula, just until all the ingredients are incorporated and a soft dough begins to form. Do not knead the dough, as this will make it elastic and difficult to shape into patties.

Flatten the dough evenly in the bottom of the bowl and divide it into 4 to 6 equal portions (depending upon how thick or thin you prefer them) with the edge of the spatula. Pick up a piece of dough, form it into a ball, and then press it flat in the palm of your hand. Put the ring mold on the lined baking sheet and put the flattened dough inside the ring mold. Press the dough to fill the ring. Remove the ring and repeat with the additional pieces of dough. If you don't have a ring mold, form the dough into a ball, press it flat on the baking sheet, and then continue to press and shape the burgers.

Drape a sheet of foil over the baking sheet and crimp the edges to seal the foil. Bake on the middle oven rack for 45 minutes.

Remove from the oven and let cool for 30 minutes with the foil cover in place. When cool enough to handle but still warm, transfer the burgers to a food storage bag. Add the ingredients for the finishing marinade (or use plain water if you don't care for smoke seasoning), press out as much air as possible, and seal the bag. Refrigerate for several hours or until most of the marinade has been absorbed before grilling.

To grill the burgers on the stove, oil a nonstick skillet or grill pan and place over medium heat. Pan sear the burgers until heated through and nicely browned on both sides. For outdoor grilling, brush or spray the grill grates with cooking oil or use a nonstick grill mat. Brush the burgers with cooking oil before broiling or outdoor grilling. Grill until heated through and grill marks appear. Avoid overgrilling since the burgers are already cooked.

Tips from Chef Skye

- Once the burgers have absorbed the marinade, they will keep in the storage bag in the refrigerator for 1 week.

- Alternatively, the uncooked burgers can be frozen for up to 3 months. Simply wrap them between layers of waxed paper or parchment paper and put them in a freezer storage bag. Thaw the burgers in the refrigerator before grilling.

Meatballs

These tender and delicious meatless meatballs are perfect for using in pasta sauce, soup, stew, or meatball sandwiches. They hold up very well in sauces, soups, and stews, unlike many commercial plant-based meatballs that tend to break down with prolonged simmering. *NOTE: The prepared Meatballs must be refrigerated for 8 hours prior to finishing to optimize their texture, so plan accordingly.*

WET INGREDIENTS

2 tablespoons **textured vegetable/soy protein granules**

2 tablespoons boiling **water**

½ cup **water**

3 tablespoons **tamari**, **soy sauce**, or **Bragg Liquid Aminos**

1 tablespoon **olive oil**

DRY INGREDIENTS

1 cup (150 g) **vital wheat gluten**

1 tablespoon **garbanzo bean flour**

1 tablespoon **mushroom powder**

1 tablespoon **dried minced onion**

2 teaspoons **onion powder**

2 teaspoons **dried parsley**

1½ teaspoons **garlic powder**

½ teaspoon coarsely ground **black pepper**

SIMMERING BROTH

12 cups **Beaf Simmering Broth** (page 56)
or commercial vegetable broth

Put the protein granules in a small bowl. Add the boiling water and let the granules rehydrate for 10 minutes.

Put the remaining wet ingredients in a standard or mini blender. Add the rehydrated granules and pulse the blender a few times to coarsely grind. The goal is to reduce the size of the granules but leave some texture (if the granules are too large, they will have a tendency to fall out of the dough when the meatballs are rolled or during the simmering process).

Pour into the dry ingredients. Mix just until the liquid is incorporated and the dry ingredients are moistened; the mixture may seem a bit dry. Do not knead the dough or the meatballs will be difficult to roll.

Pinch off a piece of dough and compress it in your hands. Roll it into a small ball between your palms (about 1½-inch diameter for large meatballs, 1-inch diameter for medium meatballs, or ¾-inch diameter for small meatballs) and set aside on a work surface. Repeat with the remaining dough. Try to work quickly when rolling; the gluten in the dough becomes more elastic the longer the dough sits, and this will make rolling more difficult.

Bring the broth to a boil. Use a slotted spoon to remove the larger solids. It's not necessary to strain the broth completely until later. Add the meatballs to the boiling broth and immediately decrease the heat to maintain a gentle simmer. Cook uncovered for 25 minutes for large meatballs, 20 minutes for medium meatballs, or 15 minutes for small meatballs.

Check frequently to maintain the broth at a very gentle simmer. Do not boil. Turn the meatballs occasionally once they float to the top of the pot.

Remove the pot from the heat and let the meatballs cool in the broth. Transfer the meatballs to a food storage bag, seal the bag, and refrigerate for 8 hours to optimize their texture before browning. Strain the simmering broth into a food storage container and refrigerate for future use.

To brown the meatballs, put 2 tablespoons of cooking oil in a nonstick skillet over medium heat. Alternatively, add them to a sauce, soup, or stew the last 15 minutes of cooking time before serving.

Meatball Seasoning Variations

- For Italian meatballs, omit the dried parsley from the dry ingredients and add 1 teaspoon dried basil, 1 teaspoon dried oregano, and ¼ teaspoon crushed red pepper flakes.

- For Mediterranean meatballs, add 1 teaspoon dried oregano and ½ teaspoon ground cumin to the dry ingredients.

- For Mexican meatballs, omit the dried parsley from the dry ingredients and add 1 teaspoon dried oregano, ½ teaspoon ground cumin, ½ teaspoon ground coriander, and ¼ teaspoon ground red chiles.

- For Moroccan meatballs, add ½ teaspoon ground cumin, ½ teaspoon ground allspice, and ¼ teaspoon ground red chiles to the dry ingredients.

- For Swedish meatballs, omit the dried parsley from the dry ingredients and add ½ teaspoon ground nutmeg and ½ teaspoon ground allspice.

Deli-Style Smoky Turky

YIELDS 2 POUNDS

This deli-style roast has a delectable smoked flavor and is a plant-based alternative to deli-style tur-key luncheon slices. The turky is made from a blend of vital wheat gluten and select seasonings. A pressure cooker is recommended for preparation; however, oven baking is an option. *NOTE: The cooked turky must be refrigerated for 8 hours before slicing to optimize its texture, so plan accordingly.* An electric slicer is recommended for creating uniform slices, which can be served hot or cold.

DRY INGREDIENTS

2 cups (300 g) **vital wheat gluten**

¼ cup **garbanzo bean flour**

2 tablespoons **onion powder**

1 tablespoon **nutritional yeast flakes**

2 teaspoons **garlic powder**

2 teaspoons coarsely ground **black pepper** (optional)

1 teaspoon **poultry seasoning** or **Aromatica** (page 161)

WET INGREDIENTS

2⅔ cups (640 ml) **water**

2 tablespoons neutral **vegetable oil**

1 tablespoon **hickory liquid smoke** (reduce or omit if sensitive to smoke flavor)

2 teaspoons **fine sea salt** or **kosher salt**

Put the dry ingredients in a large bowl and whisk to combine. Put the liquid ingredients in a medium bowl and stir to combine.

Pour the liquid ingredients into the dry ingredients and mix well. Knead the dough in the bowl with a sturdy silicone spatula to develop the gluten until some resistance can be felt in the dough, about 2 minutes.

Lay an 18-inch-long sheet of heavy-duty aluminum foil on a work surface. Put the dough on top and form it into a round mass. The dough will be very soft and wet and will tend to spread out, but try as best as you can to keep it as a round mass. Do not add more vital wheat gluten!

Before the dough begins to spread out, lift the edge of the foil over the dough and start to roll the dough inside the foil, pinching the ends closed while simulta-neously rolling. The goal is to create a thick, compact roast and not a thin sausage shape. This may take a little bit of practice, so be patient. Bend the twisted ends in half to lock them tight. Wrap in a second sheet of foil in a similar manner. If you will be oven baking the dough (rather than pressure cooking it), wrap it in a third sheet of foil for reinforcement.

To pressure cook, put 3 cups of water in the cooker and put the trivet in place. Add the package, seal the lid, close the steam valve, and cook on high for 1 hour and 45 minutes. Turn the unit off and let the pressure release naturally for 30 minutes.

To oven bake (instead of pressure cook), preheat the oven to 350 degrees F (175 degrees C). Put the package directly on the middle oven rack and bake for 2 hours.

Remove the package, let cool, then refrigerate for 8 hours to optimize the texture before slicing.

Individual
Hand-Rolled Sausages

Introduction

To create individual hand-rolled sausages, seasoned gluten dough is divided into individual portions, rolled and sealed in aluminum foil, and then cooked in a conventional steamer or pressure cooker. After they are steamed, the sausages are refrigerated for 8 hours to optimize their texture before being browned in a skillet or on the grill.

Pop-up aluminum foil (9 x 10¾ inches) is recommended for wrapping the sausages prior to steaming. Pop-up foil is commonly used in the restaurant industry for wrapping baked potatoes. It's very convenient because cutting the foil to create wrappers is not necessary.

Although pop-up foil is not available in all supermarkets, it is commonly used in hair salons for coloring hair and can be found in beauty supply stores. It can also be purchased online. Pop-up foil is very thin and flimsy, so double or triple wrapping the sausages is required so they do not burst open while steaming.

If you don't have pop-up foil, standard or heavy-duty aluminum foil can be used; however, the foil will need to be cut with scissors to create eight 8 x 10-inch wrappers. The sausages only need to be wrapped once when using standard or heavy-duty foil (unless the foil tears when you're twisting the ends).

If you don't want the dough coming into contact with aluminum foil, the dough can first be wrapped in parchment paper to create a barrier and then wrapped in the foil. The foil is required.

The sausage recipes are formulated with as much liquid as possible, beyond the point of saturation. This saturation is necessary for creating a juicy and meaty sausage. It's not uncommon to have a small amount of excess liquid remaining in the bottom of the bowl after mixing the dough.

Resist the urge to add more vital wheat gluten to absorb the extra liquid, as this will make the finished sausages dry and bread-like. However, handling and rolling the soft, wet dough in foil can be a little tricky, at least initially, so be patient when learning to wrap the sausages. Like any skill, it takes a little practice.

Meat-based sausages use a casing to contain the meat and give the sausage its shape. Plant-based sausages have no casing, and since they are hand-rolled in aluminum foil, imperfections in their appearance are to be expected. However, these surface imperfections will not detract from their excellent flavor and texture. Browning the sausages before serving actually creates a light "casing," so to speak, which significantly improves their appearance and minimizes these imperfections. If you wish to create a casing, the sausages can be wrapped with moistened rice paper (spring roll sheets). I have achieved very good results with this technique.

NOTE: *Steamed sausages must be cooled to room temperature and then refrigerated in their foil wrappers for 8 hours to firm and optimize their texture prior to finishing, so plan accordingly.*

The prepared sausages are at their best when browned in a skillet with cooking oil before serving. They are also ideal for grilling; just be sure to brush them with cooking oil to keep them moist as they grill. Don't grill the sausages over open flames; hot embers are best. Avoid overcooking the sausages, as this can cause excessive dryness.

General Preparation Instructions

Preparing the Dough

Put the dry ingredients in a large bowl and whisk to combine. Put the liquid ingredients in a separate bowl and stir to combine. Put any blender ingredients in a blender and process until the seasonings are finely ground. Pour the liquid ingredients or blender mixture into the dry ingredients and combine thoroughly with a silicone spatula to develop the gluten. For sausages that use minced fresh garlic, add the garlic to the bowl when adding the liquid or blender ingredients.

The dough will be soft and wet. This is desirable, as it will promote a moist, meaty sausage texture rather than a dry, bread-like texture. Let the dough rest for 5 minutes to allow the dry ingredients to absorb as much liquid as possible. Flatten the dough evenly in the bowl and divide it using the edge of the spatula into 6 equal portions (or 10 portions for Maple-Sage Sausage Links).

Wrapping the Dough

Put a portion of the dough on a foil square and shape it into a sausage. The dough will be very wet, so keep a moist paper towel on hand to wipe your fingers as you work. Don't worry about creating perfect sausage shapes, as the dough will expand to conform to the cylindrical shape of the foil package when it is steamed.

Roll the dough inside the foil to create a small cylinder while simultaneously pinching the ends closed. Twist the ends tightly to seal. When using pop-up foil, roll again in a second foil wrapper. If the foil should tear while you're twisting the ends, roll again in additional foil. The dough needs to be securely sealed in the foil to prevent moisture from leaking out and to prevent steam moisture from entering the packages. Repeat the process to wrap the remaining pieces of dough.

Steaming

To steam the sausages, use a large cooking pot with a lid and a steamer insert. Put enough water in the pot to just reach the bottom of the steamer insert. Do not overfill the pot or the foil packages will be sitting in water. Bring the water to a rolling boil. Put the foil packages in the steamer insert and cover the pot. The water must be boiling to generate the proper amount of steam heat to cook the sausages thoroughly and evenly. Steam for 45 minutes. Do not the let the pot boil dry! Add hot water as necessary. Remove the packages and let cool.

Pressure Cooking

To pressure cook the sausages (instead of steaming them), add 3 cups of water to the cooker and insert the trivet. Put the foil packages on the trivet, seal the lid, close the steam valve, and cook on high for 20 minutes. Turn the unit off and let the pressure subside naturally for 25 minutes. Remove the packages and let cool.

Finishing the Sausages

Refrigerate the foil packages for 8 hours in order to firm the sausages and optimize their texture before browning and serving. To brown them on the stove top, put 2 tablespoons of cooking oil in a nonstick skillet or well-seasoned cast-iron skillet over medium heat. (Although optional, a teaspoon of tamari will encourage browning.) Add the sausages and cook until nicely browned all over. Transfer to a plate lined with paper towels to blot any excess oil. The sausages are now ready to eat or use in recipes.

To grill (rather than brown on the stove top), brush the sausages with cooking oil and grill over hot embers until lightly browned or until grill marks appear. Avoid direct flames and do not overcook.

"Sweet" or "Hot" Italian Sausages

C lassic Italian seasonings give these sausages their characteristic flavor. The seasoning blend offers options for "sweet" (mild) sausages or "hot" (spicy) sausages. Note that in this recipe some of the fennel seeds are left whole (in the dry ingredients) and some are finely ground with the blender ingredients. Please review the sausage introduction (page 139) and then refer to the instructions for sausage preparation (page 140).

DRY INGREDIENTS

1 cup (150 g) **vital wheat gluten**

1 tablespoon **garbanzo bean flour**

1 tablespoon **dried minced onion**

2 teaspoons **onion powder**

1 teaspoon whole **fennel seeds**

BLENDER INGREDIENTS

1¼ cups (300 ml) **water**

2 tablespoons **tamari**, **soy sauce**, or **Bragg Liquid Aminos**

1 tablespoon **olive oil**

1 teaspoon whole **fennel seeds**

1 teaspoon **dried oregano**

1 teaspoon **dried basil**

1 teaspoon **hickory liquid smoke**

¼ teaspoon ground **white pepper** for "sweet" (mild) sausages, or 2 teaspoons crushed **red pepper flakes** for "hot" (spicy) sausages

¼ teaspoon **sea salt** or **kosher salt**

FRESH INGREDIENT

3 cloves **garlic**, minced

Bavarian Bratwurst

T hese flavorful meatless sausages are perfect for celebrating Oktoberfest, but they also are delicious any time of the year. This recipe is made with my special blend of German-inspired seasonings. Please review the sausage introduction (page 139) and then refer to the instructions for sausage preparation (page 140).

DRY INGREDIENTS

1 cup (150 g) **vital wheat gluten**

1 tablespoon **garbanzo bean flour**

1 tablespoon **onion powder**

BLENDER INGREDIENTS

1⅓ cups (320 ml) **water**

2 tablespoons mellow **white miso**

1 tablespoon neutral **vegetable oil**

¾ teaspoon **sea salt** or **kosher salt**

½ teaspoon **poultry seasoning** or **Aromatica** (page 161)

¼ teaspoon **caraway seeds**

¼ teaspoon **ground ginger**

¼ teaspoon **ground allspice**

¼ teaspoon ground **white pepper**

FRESH INGREDIENT

3 cloves **garlic**, minced

Frankfurters

My special blend of seasonings gives these plump, tasty franks their characteristic flavor. Because they're hand rolled, they're a bit rustic in appearance but delicious nonetheless. Garnish with your favorite accoutrements, such as diced onion, relish, ketchup, and/or mustard, or try topping them with veggie chili for chili dogs. Please review the sausage introduction (page 139) and then refer to the instructions for sausage preparation (page 140).

DRY INGREDIENTS

1 cup (150 g) **vital wheat gluten**

1 tablespoon **garbanzo bean flour**

1 tablespoon **onion powder**

1½ teaspoons **garlic powder**

¾ teaspoon **smoked paprika**

½ teaspoon **ground mustard**

½ teaspoon **ground coriander**

½ teaspoon **poultry seasoning** or **Aromatica**
   (page 161)

½ teaspoon **ground nutmeg**

¼ teaspoon **sea salt** or **kosher salt**

¼ teaspoon ground **white pepper**

LIQUID INGREDIENTS

1¼ cups (300 ml) **water**

2 tablespoons **tamari**, **soy sauce**, or **Bragg Liquid Aminos**

1 tablespoon neutral **vegetable oil**

2 teaspoons **hickory liquid smoke**

Andouille Sausage

Andouille sausage originated in France but was later brought to Louisiana by French immigrants. In the United States, the sausage is most often associated with Cajun cooking. Andouille sausages, which are heavily seasoned with garlic and cayenne, are sometimes referred to as "hot link" sausages. Please review the sausage introduction (page 139) and then refer to the instructions for sausage preparation (page 140).

DRY INGREDIENTS

1 cup (150 g) **vital wheat gluten**

1 tablespoon **garbanzo bean flour**

1 tablespoon **dried minced onion**

1 teaspoon **onion powder**

1 teaspoon **garlic powder**

BLENDER INGREDIENTS

1¼ cups (300 ml) **water**

2 tablespoons mellow **white miso**

1 tablespoon neutral **vegetable oil**

1 teaspoon **hickory liquid smoke**

1 teaspoon **organic sugar**

¾ teaspoon **sea salt** or **kosher salt**

½–1 teaspoon **cayenne** (use the larger amount for fiery sausages)

½ teaspoon **poultry seasoning** or **Aromatica** (page 161)

½ teaspoon **smoked paprika**

FRESH INGREDIENT

3 cloves garlic, minced

British Bangers

YIELDS 8 SHORT, PLUMP SAUSAGES

Bangers are a type of short, plump sausage common in the United Kingdom. Bangers are often an essential part of pub food, as they are quick to prepare. "Bangers and mash" (sausages with mashed potatoes and onion gravy) is a traditional British Isles favorite. The term *bangers* is attributed to the fact that sausages, particularly the kind produced during World War II under rationing, were made with water, so they were more likely to explode under high heat if not cooked carefully. Fortunately, this isn't an issue with their plant-based counterparts. If you want to serve these the traditional way, whip up a pot of mashed potatoes and top them and the bangers with Savory Onion Gravy (page 166). Please review the sausage introduction (page 139) and then refer to the instructions for sausage preparation (page 140).

DRY INGREDIENTS

1 cup (150 g) **vital wheat gluten**

1 tablespoon **garbanzo bean flour**

1 tablespoon **dried minced onion**

2 teaspoons **onion powder**

½ teaspoon coarsely ground **black pepper**

BLENDER INGREDIENTS

1¼ cups (300 ml) **water**

2 tablespoons **tamari**, **soy sauce**, or **Bragg Liquid Aminos**

1 tablespoon neutral **vegetable oil**

2 teaspoons **dried rubbed sage**

1 teaspoon freshly grated **lemon zest**

1 teaspoon **hickory liquid smoke**

½ teaspoon **ground ginger**

½ teaspoon **ground nutmeg**

¼ teaspoon **sea salt** or **kosher salt**

FRESH INGREDIENT

3 cloves **garlic**, minced

Chikun-Apple Sausages

Hints of sweet apple and savory seasonings flavor these mild and tasty chikun sausages. Please review the sausage introduction (page 139) and then refer to the instructions for sausage preparation (page 140).

DRY INGREDIENTS

1 cup (150 g) **vital wheat gluten**

2 tablespoons finely chopped **dried apple**

1 tablespoon **garbanzo bean flour**

2 teaspoons **onion powder**

½ teaspoon **garlic powder**

BLENDER INGREDIENTS

1⅓ cups (320 ml) **water**

1 tablespoon mellow **white miso**

1 tablespoon neutral **vegetable oil**

2 teaspoons **nutritional yeast flakes**

1 teaspoon **sea salt** or **kosher salt**

½ teaspoon **poultry seasoning** or **Aromatica** (page 161)

Polska Kielbasa

Kielbasa is the Polish word for "sausage." In Poland, many varieties of kielbasa exist and are seasoned differently according to region and even family. These sausages are seasoned with my own special blend of onion, black and white pepper, an abundance of fresh garlic, and other select herbs and spices. Spicy golden mustard, horseradish mustard, or Dijon mustard are ideal condiments to serve with kielbasa. Please review the sausage introduction (page 139) and then refer to the instructions for sausage preparation (page 140).

DRY INGREDIENTS

1 cup (150 g) **vital wheat gluten**

1 tablespoon **garbanzo bean flour**

1 tablespoon **dried minced onion**

2 teaspoons **onion powder**

½ teaspoon coarsely ground **black pepper**

BLENDER INGREDIENTS

1¼ cups (300 ml) **water**

2 tablespoons **tamari**, **soy sauce**, or **Bragg Liquid Aminos**

1 tablespoon neutral **vegetable oil**

2 teaspoons **hickory liquid smoke**

1 teaspoon **summer savory or dried marjoram**

½ teaspoon ground **white pepper**

¼ teaspoon **ground allspice**

¼ teaspoon **sea salt** or **kosher salt**

FRESH INGREDIENT

4 cloves **garlic**, minced

Maple-Sage Sausage Links

The wonderful flavors of rubbed sage and maple syrup complement these tasty breakfast sausages. They're perfect served alongside eggless scrambles, pancakes, or French toast. Please review the sausage introduction (page 139) and then refer to the instructions for sausage preparation (page 140).

DRY INGREDIENTS

1 cup (150 g) **vital wheat gluten**

1 tablespoon **garbanzo bean flour**

1 tablespoon **dried minced onion**

2 teaspoons **onion powder**

¼ teaspoon coarsely ground **black pepper**

BLENDER INGREDIENTS

1 cup plus 2 tablespoons (270 ml) **water**

2 tablespoons **tamari**, **soy sauce**, or **Bragg Liquid Aminos**

2 tablespoons **real maple syrup**

1 tablespoon neutral **vegetable oil**

2 teaspoons **dried rubbed sage**

½ teaspoon **poultry seasoning** or **Aromatica** (page 161)

½ teaspoon **paprika**

½ teaspoon **ground nutmeg**

¼ teaspoon **ground red pepper** or **cayenne**

¼ teaspoon **sea salt** or **kosher salt**

FRESH INGREDIENT

3 cloves **garlic**, minced

Breakfast Sausage Patties

 savory American-style breakfast sausage flavored with onion, garlic, sage, thyme, and black pepper, with a hint of nutmeg.

WET INGREDIENTS

2 tablespoons **textured vegetable/soy protein granules**

2 tablespoons boiling **water**

¾ cup (180 ml) **water**

2 tablespoons **tamari**, **soy sauce**, or **Bragg Liquid Aminos**

1 tablespoon neutral **vegetable oil**

3 cloves **garlic**, minced

¼ teaspoon **sea salt** or **kosher salt**

DRY INGREDIENTS

1 cup (150 g) **vital wheat gluten**

1 tablespoon **dried minced onion**

2 teaspoons **onion powder**

2 teaspoons **mushroom powder**

2 teaspoons **dried rubbed sage**

½ teaspoon **dried thyme**

½ teaspoon coarsely ground **black pepper**

½ teaspoon **ground nutmeg**

Put the protein granules in a small bowl. Add the boiling water and let the granules rehydrate for 10 minutes.

Put the water, tamari, oil, garlic, and salt in a separate small bowl and stir to combine. Stir in the rehydrated protein granules. Set aside.

Preheat the oven to 350 degrees F (175 degrees C). Put a stainless-steel cooling rack on a baking sheet and line the rack with parchment paper or a silicone baking mat. The cooling rack is not required but is recommended, as it will prevent the excessive browning that would occur from direct contact with the hot baking sheet.

Put the dry ingredients in a large bowl and whisk until well combined. Give the wet ingredients a quick stir and then pour all at once into the dry ingredients. Fold the mixture together with a sturdy silicone spatula just until all ingredients are incorporated and a dough begins to form. Do not knead the dough, as this will make it elastic and difficult to shape into patties.

Flatten the dough evenly in the bottom of the bowl and divide it into 8 equal portions with the edge of the spatula. Pick up a piece of dough, form it into a ball, and then press it flat on the baking sheet. Repeat with the remaining dough. If any of the protein granules fall out, press them back into the patties as best as you can.

Drape a sheet of foil over the baking sheet and crimp the edges to seal the foil. Bake on the middle oven rack for 40 minutes.

Remove from the oven and let the patties cool for 20 minutes with the foil cover in place. When cool enough to handle, transfer the patties to a food storage bag or container. Add 2 tablespoons of water for moisture. Seal the bag and refrigerate until the patties are chilled (this will firm and enhance their texture before they are browned and served).

To brown, put 2 tablespoons of cooking oil in a nonstick skillet and place over medium heat. Cook until the patties are golden brown on both sides.

SAUSAGE CRUMBLES: Put 2 tablespoons of cooking oil in a nonstick skillet and place over medium heat. Crumble the chilled patties into the skillet and brown in the hot oil. Use in recipes as desired.

Hard Sausages

Pepperoni

P epperoni is an Italian hard sausage richly seasoned with onion and garlic, crushed red pepper, smoked paprika, and fennel seeds. A pressure cooker is recommended for preparation; however, oven baking is an option. *NOTE: Hard Sausages must be refrigerated for 8 hours prior to serving to optimize the texture, so plan accordingly.*

1 cup (150 g) **vital wheat gluten**

½ cup (120 ml) **water**

3 tablespoons **olive oil**

3 tablespoons **tamari**, **soy sauce**, or **Bragg Liquid Aminos**

2 tablespoons **tomato paste**

2 teaspoons **red wine vinegar** or **apple cider vinegar**

2 teaspoons **smoked paprika**

2 teaspoons **organic sugar**

2 teaspoons whole **fennel seeds**

1 teaspoon **crushed red pepper flakes** (more or less as desired)

1 teaspoon **ground mustard**

4 cloves **garlic**, minced

Put the vital wheat gluten in a large bowl.

Put the water, oil, tamari, tomato paste, vinegar, smoked paprika, sugar, fennel seeds, red pepper flakes, and ground mustard in a blender and process until the fennel seeds are coarsely ground. Pour into the vital wheat gluten, add the garlic, and combine thoroughly with a sturdy silicone spatula to form a dough. Knead the dough in the bowl until it exhibits some elasticity, about 1 minute. Divide the dough in half.

Lay a 12-inch-long sheet of heavy-duty aluminum foil on a work surface. Shape one portion of the dough into a slender log about 6 inches long and place it near the edge of the foil. Lift the edge of the foil over the dough and begin rolling into a tight cylinder. Twist the ends tightly to seal. Bend the ends in half to lock them tight. Wrap in a second sheet of foil in the same manner. Repeat the shaping and double-wrapping technique with the second portion of dough. If you will be oven baking the dough (rather than pressure cooking it), wrap each package in a third sheet of foil for reinforcement.

To pressure cook, put 3 cups of water in the cooker and put the trivet in place. Add the packages, seal the lid, close the steam valve, and cook on high for 1 hour. Turn the unit off and let the pressure release naturally for 30 minutes.

To oven bake (instead of pressure cook), preheat the oven to 325 degrees F (170 degrees C). Put the packages directly on the middle oven rack and bake for 1 hour and 15 minutes.

Remove the packages and let cool. Then refrigerate the packages for 8 hours to optimize the texture and make thin slicing easier. The pepperoni is ready to eat or use in recipes; it does not require any additional finishing. Slice thick or thin and use as needed.

VARIATION: For individual snack-sized pepperoni sausages, or *pepperettes*, divide the dough into 6 equal portions. Wrap and steam the dough for 45 minutes (follow the instructions on pages 140–141 for Individual Hand-Rolled Sausages).

Hard Salami

Traditional meat-based salami is a cured, fermented, and air-dried sausage. This presented some fundamental problems for creating a plant-based version. In spite of these challenges, and the few extra steps involved in preparation, I feel this recipe offers a very satisfying plant-based version of traditional meat salami. A pressure cooker is recommended for preparation; however, oven baking is an option. *NOTE: Hard Salami must be refrigerated for 8 hours prior to serving to optimize the texture, so plan accordingly.*

LIGHT MARBLING DOUGH

⅓ cup (50 g) **vital wheat gluten**

1 teaspoon **onion powder**

¼ cup (60 ml) **water**

2 teaspoons **olive oil**

½ teaspoon **sea salt** or **kosher salt**

DARK MARBLING DOUGH

1 cup (150 g) **vital wheat gluten**

2 teaspoons **onion powder**

2 teaspoons cracked **black pepper**

1 teaspoon **garlic powder**

½ cup (120 ml) **water**

2 tablespoons **tamari**, **soy sauce**, or **Bragg Liquid Aminos**

2 tablespoons **olive oil**

2 tablespoons **tomato paste**

1 tablespoon **red miso**, or 1½ teaspoons **tamari** and 1½ teaspoons **tomato paste**

2 teaspoons **red wine vinegar** or **apple cider vinegar**

1 teaspoon **organic sugar**

1 teaspoon **hickory liquid smoke**

½ teaspoon **browning liquid** (color enhancer)

ADDITIONAL INGREDIENTS

3 cloves **garlic**, minced

Tapioca **flour/starch**, **unmodified potato starch**, or **cornstarch**

To prepare the light marbling dough, put the vital wheat gluten and onion powder in a small bowl and stir to combine. Put the water, oil, and salt in a separate bowl or measuring cup and stir until the salt dissolves. Pour into the vital wheat gluten mixture and mix thoroughly with a sturdy silicone spatula to form a dough. Wrap the small mass of dough securely in aluminum foil (shaping the dough is not important).

To pressure cook, put 3 cups of water in the cooker and put the trivet in place. Add the small package of light marbling dough, seal the lid, close the steam valve, and cook on high for 30 minutes. Turn the cooker off and release the steam. Remove the package and let cool until it can be handled comfortably. Do not empty the water from the cooker as it will be used again shortly.

To oven bake (rather than pressure cook), preheat the oven to 350 degrees F (175 degrees C). Place the package directly on the middle oven rack and bake for 30 minutes. Remove the package and let cool until it can be handled comfortably.

Mince the cooked gluten and set aside while you prepare the dough for the dark marbling.

To prepare the dark marbling dough, put the vital wheat gluten, onion powder, pepper, and garlic powder in a large bowl and whisk to combine. Put the water, tamari, oil, tomato paste, miso, vinegar, sugar, liquid smoke, and browning liquid in a small bowl and whisk until the miso and sugar are dissolved. Stir the cooked minced gluten and fresh garlic into the wet ingredients. Pour into the dry ingredients and combine thoroughly with a sturdy silicone spatula. Knead the dough in the bowl until it exhibits some elasticity, about 1 minute.

Lay an 18-inch-long sheet of heavy-duty aluminum foil on a work surface. Shape the dough into an 8-inch log and place it near the edge of the foil. Lift the edge of the foil over the dough and begin rolling into a tight cylinder. Twist the ends tightly to seal. Bend the twisted ends in half to lock them tight. Wrap in a second sheet of foil in the same manner. If you will be oven baking the dough (instead of pressure cooking it), wrap it in a third sheet of foil for reinforcement.

To pressure cook, make sure there is sufficient water in the cooker. Add the package, seal the lid, close the steam valve, and cook on high for 1 hour and 15 minutes. Turn the cooker off and let the pressure release naturally for 30 minutes. Remove the package and let cool.

To oven bake (rather than pressure cook), preheat the oven to 350 degrees F (175 degrees C). Place the package directly on the middle oven rack and bake for 1 hour and 30 minutes. Remove the package and let cool.

To finish the salami, refrigerate the package for 8 hours to optimize the texture and make thin slicing easier.

Sprinkle some starch on a plate or work surface and roll the salami in the starch thoroughly and evenly, shaking off any excess. The salami is now ready to be sliced very thin (an electric slicer is ideal).

Seasoning Blends and Rubs

Aromatica

An alternative to commercial poultry seasoning.

2 tablespoons **rubbed sage**

2 tablespoons **dried thyme**

2 tablespoons **dried marjoram**

2 tablespoons **dried rosemary**, or 1 teaspoon **ground rosemary**

1 teaspoon **celery seeds**

1 teaspoon ground **white pepper**

Put all the ingredients in a spice grinder or dry blender and process until finely powdered. Store in an airtight container at room temperature and use within 6 months.

Berbere Spice Blend

This aromatic and peppery blend of traditional berbere spices is commonly used in Ethiopian cooking. To use, rub prepared Chikun Drumsticks or Drumettes (page 22) with cooking oil and then generously rub with the spice blend prior to grilling. It's also sublime used as a rub or seasoning for Ethiopian-style beaf, vegetables, or rice.

4 tablespoons (¼ cup) **paprika**

1 tablespoon **onion powder**

1 tablespoon **garlic powder**

2 teaspoons **ground fenugreek**

2 teaspoons **cayenne**

1½ teaspoons **ground cumin**

1½ teaspoons **ground turmeric**

1½ teaspoons coarsely ground **black pepper**

¾ teaspoon **ground cardamom**

¾ teaspoon **ground coriander**

½ teaspoon **ground cloves**

¼ teaspoon **ground cinnamon**

Put all the ingredients in an airtight container, seal, and shake well. Store at room temperature and use within 6 months.

Garam Masala (INDIAN SPICE BLEND)

 fragrant blend of exotic spices commonly used in Indian cuisine.

2 tablespoons **ground coriander**

2 tablespoons **ground turmeric**

1 tablespoon **ground ginger**

2 teaspoons **ground cinnamon**

2 teaspoons **ground cloves**

2 teaspoons **ground nutmeg**

1 teaspoon coarsely ground **black pepper**

1 teaspoon **ground cardamom** (optional)

Put all the ingredients in a small bowl and stir until well combined. Store in an airtight container at room temperature and use within 6 months.

Montreal Seasoning

This flavorful blend is wonderful for seasoning Steak Medallions or Cutlets (page 57) before grilling. Try it for seasoning portobello mushrooms or wedge fries made from russet potatoes or sweet potatoes.

¼ cup coarse **sea salt** or **kosher salt**

2 tablespoons whole **black peppercorns** or **mixed peppercorns**

2 tablespoons **dried minced or flaked onion**

1 tablespoon **dried rosemary**, or ½ teaspoon ground rosemary

2 teaspoons **garlic powder**

2 teaspoons whole **fennel seeds**

2 teaspoons **dried thyme**

1 teaspoon **smoked paprika**

½ teaspoon ground **dried orange peel**

Put all the ingredients in a spice grinder or dry blender and process until finely ground. Store in an airtight container at room temperature and use within 6 months.

Jamaican Jerk Spice

Jerk is a style of cooking native to Jamaica in which chicken or pork is dry rubbed or wet marinated with a very hot spice mixture called Jamaican jerk spice. For our purposes, it is used as a fiery seasoning for chikun and porq.

2 tablespoons **onion powder**

1 tablespoon **dried thyme**

1 tablespoon **ground allspice**

1 tablespoon **sea salt** or **kosher salt**

1 tablespoon **organic sugar**

2 teaspoons coarsely ground **black pepper**

2 teaspoons **cayenne**

2 teaspoons **garlic powder**

½ teaspoon grated **nutmeg**

½ teaspoon **ground cinnamon**

Put all the ingredients in a small bowl and stir to combine. Store in an airtight container at room temperature and use within 6 months.

Tips from Chef Skye

- For shredded Jamaican jerk chikun or porq, rub the dough with 1 tablespoon of the spice mixture prior to baking.

- For prepared Chikun Drumsticks or Drumettes (page 22), rub the chikun with cooking oil and then generously rub with the spice mixture prior to grilling.

Cajun Dry Rub

ajun dry rub is a spicy hot seasoning inspired by the cuisine of Louisiana. Use it as a spicy rub for chikun and porq.

3 tablespoons **coarse sea salt** or **kosher salt**

3 tablespoons **paprika**

1 tablespoon **onion powder**

1 tablespoon **garlic powder**

1 tablespoon **dried thyme**

1 tablespoon **dried oregano**

2 teaspoons coarsely ground **black pepper**

2 teaspoons **cayenne**

1 **bay leaf**, crumbled

Put all the ingredients in a dry blender and process until the bay leaf is completely powdered. Store the mixture in an airtight container at room temperature and use within 6 months.

Tips from Chef Skye

- For shredded Cajun chikun or porq, rub the dough with 1 tablespoon of the spice mixture prior to baking.

- For prepared Chikun Drumsticks or Drumettes (page 22) or Porq Chops (page 94), rub the pieces with cooking oil and then generously rub with the spice mixture prior to grilling.

Gravies, Sauces, and Glazes

Savory Onion Gravy

 savory gravy flavored with vegetable broth and caramelized onions.

2 tablespoons **olive oil**

2 medium **onions**, peeled, halved, and thinly sliced

1 teaspoon **organic sugar**

Sea salt or **kosher salt**

2 tablespoons **nondairy butter** or **margarine**

¼ cup **all-purpose flour**

2 cups **Porq Simmering Broth** (page 93) or commercial vegetable broth

1 teaspoon **dark balsamic vinegar**

½ teaspoon **dried thyme**

Coarsely ground **black pepper**

Put the oil in a medium saucepan over medium heat. Add the onions, sugar, and a pinch of salt. Sauté until the onions are very tender and golden brown. Add the butter and stir until melted.

Sprinkle in the flour and stir until a thick paste forms (roux). Cook until the flour is golden and emits a nutty aroma, about 2 minutes. The flour will stick to the bottom of the saucepan, but don't worry, as it will release when the broth is incorporated.

Incorporate the broth in several increments, stirring well after each addition. Add the vinegar and thyme, increase the heat to medium-high, and bring to a boil, stirring frequently. Decrease the heat to medium-low and simmer for about 5 minutes.

Ladle half of the mixture into a blender and put the lid in place. For safety, cover the lid with a dish towel, hold down firmly, and start the blender on low speed. Gradually increase the speed and process until the gravy is smooth. Pour back into the saucepan and season with salt and pepper to taste. Cover and keep warm over low heat until ready to serve, stirring occasionally.

Hearty Brown Gravy

his broth-based gravy has a traditional beefy flavor.

2 tablespoons **olive oil**

2 tablespoons **nondairy butter** or **margarine**

¼ cup **all-purpose flour**

2 cups **Beaf Simmering Broth** (page 56)

Browning liquid (color enhancer)

Sea salt or **kosher salt**

Coarsely ground **black pepper**

Put the oil in a small saucepan over medium heat. Add the butter and stir until it is melted.

Whisk in the flour to create a thick paste (roux). Cook until the flour is golden and emits a nutty aroma, about 2 minutes. The flour will stick to the bottom of the saucepan, but don't worry, as it will release when the broth is incorporated.

Incorporate the broth in increments while vigorously stirring. Add small amounts of browning liquid as needed for depth of color. Bring to a simmer and continue to stir until the mixture thickens. Season with salt and pepper to taste. Cover and keep warm over low heat until ready to serve, stirring occasionally.

Jus

*J*us (pronounced *zhoo*) is French for "juice," and *au jus* literally means "with (its own) juice." In American cuisine, the term generally refers to a thin, light gravy or broth, which may be served with the food or placed on the side for dipping.

1 tablespoon **olive oil**

1 **shallot**, minced, or 2 tablespoons minced red onion

2 teaspoons **all-purpose flour**

2 cups **Beaf Simmering Broth** (page 56)

2 tablespoons **dry sherry** (optional)

Put the oil in a medium saucepan over medium heat. Add the shallot and sauté until tender.

Decrease the heat to low and whisk in the flour until a smooth paste forms (roux). Cook until the flour emits a nutty aroma, about 1 minute.

Incorporate the broth in increments while vigorously whisking the mixture until smooth.

Whisk in the optional sherry. Increase the heat to medium and briefly bring the gravy to a boil, stirring frequently. Cover and keep warm over low heat until ready to serve, stirring occasionally.

Golden Gravy

his creamy sauce is reminiscent of chicken gravy.

2 tablespoons neutral **vegetable oil**

2 tablespoons **nondairy butter** or **margarine**

¼ cup **all-purpose flour**

2 cups **Chikun Simmering Broth** (page 16)

Sea salt or **kosher salt**

Coarsely ground **black pepper**

Put the oil in a small saucepan over medium heat. Add the butter and stir until melted. Whisk in the flour to create a thick paste (roux). Cook until the flour is golden and emits a nutty aroma, about 2 minutes. The flour will stick to the bottom of the saucepan, but don't worry, as it will release when the broth is incorporated.

Incorporate the broth in increments while vigorously stirring. Bring to a simmer and continue to stir until the mixture thickens. Season with salt and pepper to taste. Cover and keep warm over low heat until ready to serve, stirring occasionally.

Amber Waves of Gravy

This recipe produces a velvety smooth and savory gravy that is superb for serving over slices of Holiday Roast Turky (page 120), mashed potatoes, and dressing. It also makes a terrific gravy for open-faced hot turky sandwiches.

2 tablespoons **olive oil**

2 tablespoons **nondairy butter** or **margarine**

¼ cup **all-purpose flour**

2 cups **Turky Simmering Broth** (page 123)

1 teaspoon **Worcestershire Sauce** (page 182) or commercial vegan equivalent

½ teaspoon **browning liquid** (color enhancer)

¼ teaspoon **dried thyme**

Sea salt or **kosher salt**

Coarsely ground **black pepper**

Put the oil in a medium saucepan over medium-low heat. Add the butter and stir until melted. Whisk in the flour to create a thick paste (roux). Cook until the flour is golden and emits a nutty aroma, about 2 minutes. The flour will stick to the bottom of the saucepan, but don't worry, as it will release when the broth is incorporated.

Incorporate the broth in increments while vigorously whisking to eliminate lumps. Initially the mixture will be very thick and pasty and some of the flour may begin to brown and stick to the bottom of the saucepan. This is normal and will resolve as you continue to add the broth. When the mixture has thinned a bit and is very smooth, it's safe to pour in the remaining stock.

Add the Worcestershire Sauce, browning liquid, and thyme. Continue to cook and stir until the mixture just begins to come to a boil. Decrease the heat to maintain a gentle simmer and cook uncovered, stirring frequently, until the gravy thickens. Season with salt and pepper to taste. Cover and keep warm over low heat until ready to serve, stirring occasionally.

Mushroom Gravy

This creamy gravy is heavenly served over breaded and fried chikun or porq cutlets, and divine ladled over mashed potatoes.

2 tablespoons **olive oil**

8 ounces **white or cremini mushrooms**, sliced or chopped

2 tablespoons **nondairy butter** or **margarine**

¼ cup **all-purpose flour**

1½ cups **Chikun Simmering Broth** (page 16)

½ teaspoon **dried thyme**

½ cup plain **nondairy milk**

Sea salt or **kosher salt**

Coarsely ground **black pepper**

Put the oil in a large saucepan over medium heat. Add the mushrooms and sauté until the liquid has evaporated and the mushrooms begin to brown, about 5 minutes. Stir in the butter until melted. Sprinkle in the flour and stir until a thick paste forms (roux).

Cook until the flour is golden and emits a nutty aroma, about 2 minutes. The flour will stick to the bottom of the saucepan, but don't worry, as it will release when the broth is incorporated.

Incorporate the broth in increments, stirring well after each addition. Add the thyme and bring the mixture to a boil, stirring frequently. Decrease the heat to maintain a simmer and cook for 5 minutes.

Add the milk and return to a gentle simmer. Season with salt and pepper to taste. Cover and keep warm over low heat until ready to serve, stirring occasionally.

Peppercorn-Herb Gravy

An elegant brown gravy flavored with marjoram, thyme, and peppercorns. It's lovely spooned over grilled Porq Chops or Cutlets (page 94), as well as beaf, mashed potatoes, or rice.

2 tablespoons **olive oil**

2 tablespoons **nondairy butter** or **margarine**

¼ cup **all-purpose flour**

2 cups **Porq Simmering Broth** (page 93)

2 teaspoons cracked **green or black peppercorns**

1 teaspoon **dried marjoram**

1 teaspoon **browning liquid** (color enhancer)

½ teaspoon **dried thyme**

Sea salt or **kosher salt**

Coarsely ground **black pepper**

2 tablespoons chopped **fresh parsley**

Put the oil in a small saucepan and place over medium heat. Add the butter and stir until melted. Whisk in the flour to create a thick paste (roux). Cook until the flour is golden and emits a nutty aroma, about 2 minutes. The flour will stick to the bottom of the saucepan, but don't worry, as it will release when the broth is incorporated.

Incorporate the broth in increments while vigorously stirring. Add the cracked peppercorns, marjoram, browning liquid, and thyme. Bring to a simmer and continue to stir until the mixture thickens, about 1 minute. Season with salt and pepper to taste.

Cover and keep warm over low heat until ready to serve, stirring occasionally. Stir in the parsley just before serving.

Golden Cheddar Sauce

This velvety cheese sauce has a mild Cheddar flavor that will please the entire family. It's ideal for topping hot roast beaf sandwiches, such as Philadelphia cheesesteak, or for preparing macaroni and cheese or cheesy rice. Try pouring it over steamed fresh vegetables or baked potatoes.

1¾ cups plain **nondairy milk**

5 tablespoons **tapioca flour/starch**

¼ cup neutral **vegetable oil**

¼ cup **nutritional yeast flakes**

1 tablespoon mellow **white miso**

1 tablespoon **tomato paste**

2 teaspoons **apple cider vinegar**

1 teaspoon **fine sea salt** or **kosher salt**

½ teaspoon **dry mustard**

½ teaspoon **onion powder**

Put all the ingredients in a small saucepan and whisk until smooth. Cook over medium-low heat, stirring constantly with a flexible spatula, until the mixture comes to a simmer and is bubbly, thickened, smooth, and glossy. Note that the golden color will develop as the cheese sauce cooks. Season with additional salt to taste. Cover and keep warm over low heat until ready to serve, stirring occasionally.

Chef's Best Alfredo Sauce

Alfredo sauce is a rich, creamy white sauce that's ideal for tossing with slices of pan-grilled Chi-kun Cutlets and serving over hot cooked pasta. Dairy Parmesan cheese is a primary ingredient in traditional Alfredo sauce. However, nondairy Parmesan won't provide the same texture and rich-ness; therefore, nondairy Parmesan is reserved for garnishing the finished dish and is optional.

This sauce is very easy to prepare and achieves the ideal nappe consistency (coats the back of a spoon) for serving over pasta with pan-grilled, sautéed, or steamed vegetables.

2 cups plain **nondairy milk**

1½ ounces (43 g) **raw cashews** (do not presoak)

¼ cup **olive oil**

1 tablespoon **nutritional yeast flakes**

1 tablespoon mellow **white miso**

1½ teaspoons **onion powder**

1 teaspoon **garlic powder**

1 teaspoon **fine sea salt** or **kosher salt**

¼ teaspoon ground **white pepper**

Nondairy **Parmesan**, for garnish

2 tablespoons chopped **fresh parsley**, for garnish

Put the milk, cashews, oil, nutritional yeast, miso, onion powder, garlic powder, salt, and pepper in a blender and process on high speed for 2 minutes. Strain through a fine-mesh sieve into a medium saucepan and cook over medium-low heat, stirring slowly and continually, until the mixture just comes to a simmer. Season with additional salt to taste. Cover and keep warm over low heat until ready to serve, stirring occasionally. Garnish with Parmesan and the parsley just before serving.

Horsey Sauce

 classic, zesty sauce for Prime Cut Roast Beaf (page 68) and other beaf-based dishes and sandwiches.

½ cup **No-Eggy Mayo** (page 186) or commercial vegan mayonnaise

¼ cup prepared **white horseradish** (not creamed)

¼ cup **Instant Sour Cream** (page 188) or commercial nondairy equivalent

2 tablespoons freshly squeezed **lemon juice**

Put all the ingredients in a small bowl and whisk until smooth and creamy. Transfer to a sealable container and refrigerate for 1 to 2 hours before serving to allow the flavors to blend. Use within 1 week.

Greek Tzatziki Sauce

 reek tzatziki is a tangy yogurt-and-cucumber sauce used as a condiment for Greek and other Mediterranean cuisines. This is my variation of the traditional sauce.

½ **English cucumber**, peeled, halved lengthwise, seeds removed

½ cup plain **nondairy yogurt**

1 tablespoon extra-virgin **olive oil**

2 tablespoons minced **sweet yellow onion**

1 tablespoon **red wine vinegar** or **apple cider vinegar**

2 cloves **garlic**, minced

1 teaspoon minced **fresh dill**

½ teaspoon **fine sea salt** or **kosher salt**

¼ teaspoon coarsely ground **black pepper**

Grate the cucumber on the largest holes of a box grater. Put it in a fine sieve and gently press with the back of a spoon to remove the excess juice.

Put the yogurt in a small bowl and whisk in the oil until emulsified. Stir in the cucumber, onion, vinegar, garlic, dill, salt, and pepper. Season with additional salt and pepper to taste. Refrigerate for at least 2 hours before serving to allow the flavors to blend.

Chimichurri Sauce

Chimichurri is an aromatic herb sauce that originated in Argentina and is traditionally used for grilled meat. In vegan cooking, it can be used as a sauce for dressing a wide variety of meat alternatives, such as shredded beaf or grilled seitan, chikun, tofu, tempeh, portobello mushrooms, or cauliflower steaks. It's also wonderful as a dip for crusty bread or for marinating cooked beans.

2 cups chopped **flat leaf parsley**, lightly packed

½ cup extra-virgin **olive oil**

½ cup **roasted red peppers**, skin removed, plus more for garnish

¼ cup chopped **fresh oregano**, lightly packed, or 4 teaspoons dried oregano

¼ cup **water**

¼ cup **white wine vinegar** or **champagne vinegar**

2 tablespoons **red wine vinegar**

1 **shallot**, chopped

2 cloves **garlic**, chopped

1 teaspoon minced **habanero or jalapeño chile**

1 teaspoon **sea salt** or **kosher salt**

1 teaspoon **sweet paprika**

¼ teaspoon **ground cumin**

Put all the ingredients in a food processor and process until the sauce is fairly smooth but retains a little bit of texture. Store in an airtight container in the refrigerator until ready to use. Shake well before using to emulsify.

Tangy Barbecue Sauce

A rich, thick, and tangy tomato-based sauce for grilling or broiling seitan and other meat alternatives.

¼ cup (2 ounces) **nondairy butter** or **margarine**

6 cloves **garlic**, minced

1 can (6 ounces) **tomato paste**

½ cup **dark brown sugar**

½ cup **water**

¼ cup **apple cider vinegar**

1 tablespoon **dried minced onion**

1 tablespoon **Worcestershire Sauce** (page 182) or commercial vegan equivalent

1 tablespoon **hickory liquid smoke**

1 teaspoon **fine sea salt** or **kosher salt**

1 teaspoon **Dijon or spicy mustard**

½ teaspoon **hot red pepper sauce**

Put the butter in a small saucepan over medium-low heat until melted. Add the garlic and sauté for 1 minute. Whisk in the tomato paste, sugar, water, vinegar, dried onion, Worcestershire Sauce, liquid smoke, salt, mustard, and red pepper sauce. Bring to a simmer, decrease the heat to low, and cook uncovered, stirring occasionally, until the sauce is thickened, about 1 hour. Let cool. Refrigerate to further thicken before using.

JACK D'S BARBECUE SAUCE: Replace the water with high-quality whiskey or bourbon.

Barbacoa Sauce

Barbacoa is a spicy Tex-Mex barbecue sauce that is superb when tossed with chunks or shreds of Beaf Brisket (page 74) and served with tortillas, salsa, and guacamole.

2 cups **Beaf Simmering Broth** (page 56)

¼ cup **apple cider vinegar**

¼ cup freshly squeezed **lime juice**

1 can (7 ounces) **chipotle chiles** in adobo sauce

8 cloves **garlic**

2 teaspoons **ground cumin**

2 teaspoons **dried oregano**

½ teaspoon **ground cloves**

Sea salt or **kosher salt**

Put the broth, vinegar, lime juice, chiles, garlic, cumin, oregano, and cloves in a blender and process until smooth. Transfer to a medium saucepan and bring to a gentle simmer over medium heat. Simmer uncovered until the sauce is reduced to 2 cups, about 45 minutes. Season with salt to taste.

Tips from Chef Skye ■ Chipotle chiles in adobo sauce pack a fiery heat. For a milder sauce, use a smaller amount.

Island Teriyaki Sauce and Glaze

This classic sauce and glaze hales from Asia and the Pacific Islands. It is superb for brushing on meatless meats during grilling or broiling.

2 teaspoons **cornstarch** or **unmodified potato starch**

1 tablespoon **cooking oil**

3 cloves **garlic**, minced

2 teaspoons grated **fresh ginger** (see page 31)

⅔ cup **unsweetened pineapple juice**

⅓ cup **light brown sugar**

⅓ cup **tamari**, **soy sauce**, or **Bragg Liquid Aminos**

Put the starch in a small dish. Add 1 tablespoon of water and stir to dissolve the starch and create a slurry. Set aside.

Heat the oil in a small saucepan over medium-low heat. Don't get the oil too hot. Add the garlic and ginger and cook for 30 seconds. Quickly add the pineapple juice before the garlic scorches. Add the starch slurry, brown sugar, and tamari. Whisk well to combine. Increase the heat to medium and simmer, stirring constantly, for 2 to 3 minutes. Remove from the heat and set aside. The sauce will thicken into a syrupy glaze as it cools.

ISLAND FIRE SAUCE: Stir in 1 to 2 tablespoons hot red pepper sauce when adding the tamari.

Char Siu Glaze

An aromatic, bright-red glaze for Chinese-style ribz (see page 109). Technically, *char siu*, which literally means "fork roast" (*char* meaning "fork" and *siu* meaning "roast"), refers to the traditional cooking method rather than referring to the glaze itself. Brush the ribz generously with the glaze when grilling.

½ cup **light brown sugar**

¼ cup **water**

¼ cup **tamari**, **soy sauce**, or **Bragg Liquid Aminos**

¼ cup **mirin** (Japanese sweet rice wine)

¼ cup **rice vinegar**

1 tablespoon **toasted sesame oil**

1 tablespoon grated **fresh ginger** (see page 31)

1 teaspoon **onion powder**

1 teaspoon **garlic powder**

1 teaspoon **Chinese Five Spice powder**

1 teaspoon **Asian red chile sauce** (such as sambal oelek or sriracha sauce)

1 tablespoon **beet powder**, or 1 small peeled and shredded **raw beet**

Put the brown sugar, water, tarmari, mirin, vinegar, oil, ginger, onion powder, garlic powder, Chinese Five Spice, and chile sauce in a small saucepan. Bring to a gentle simmer over medium-low heat. Cook uncovered for 20 minutes.

Remove from the heat and let cool for 10 minutes. Stir in the beet powder and let cool for 20 minutes. If shredded beet was used, strain the mixture into a container, using the back of a spoon to press and extract as much of the liquid as possible. The mixture will thicken into a syrupy glaze as it cools. Store the glaze in a sealable container in the refrigerator until ready to use.

Worcestershire Sauce

his is my signature plant-based version of the classic condiment. It's an essential ingredient for preparing Beaf (page 55) and Beaf Simmering Broth (page 56). Traditional commercial Worcestershire sauce contains anchovy paste and is therefore not suitable for people who adhere to a plant-based diet. Using the optional wakame flakes in this recipe will help replicate that flavor. I use this condiment so frequently that I often double the recipe.

1½ cups **apple cider vinegar**

1 medium **onion**, chopped

½ cup **dark balsamic vinegar**

½ cup **tamari, soy sauce**, or **Bragg Liquid Aminos**

3 tablespoons **dark brown sugar**

3 cloves **garlic**, crushed

1 piece (1½ inches) **fresh ginger**, peeled and sliced

1 strip (2 inches) **lemon peel**

1 strip (2 inches) **orange peel**

1 teaspoon **hickory liquid smoke**

1 teaspoon whole **cloves**

1 teaspoon whole **black peppercorns**

1 teaspoon **Dijon or spicy mustard**

1 **bay leaf**

Pinch dried **wakame flakes** (optional)

Put all the ingredients in a medium saucepan and bring to a boil over medium-high heat. Decrease the heat to medium-low to maintain a rapid simmer and cook until the sauce is reduced by half its volume, 30 to 40 minutes. Let cool, then press and strain through a fine-mesh sieve or a double layer of cheesecloth into a jar with a lid. Store the sauce in the refrigerator and use within 3 months.

Instant Chikun Bouillon Powder

his convenient instant bouillon powder can be used to prepare a comforting and savory chikun broth by the cup or quart. It can also be used as a quick alternative to the Chikun Simmering Broth (page 16). *Bouillon* is the French word for "broth."

1 cup **nutritional yeast flakes**

5 tablespoons **sea salt** or **kosher salt**

¼ cup **onion powder**

3 tablespoons **organic sugar**

1 tablespoon **poultry seasoning** or **Aromatica** (page 161)

1 tablespoon **garlic powder**

1 tablespoon **dried celery flakes**

¼ teaspoon ground **white pepper**

Put all the ingredients in a dry blender and process until finely powdered. Store in an airtight container at room temperature for up to 6 months.

How to Use Instant Chikun Bouillon Powder

- For a soothing mug of golden chikun broth, dissolve 1 level teaspoon bouillon powder (or more to taste) in 8 ounces of piping-hot water. Stir well. A fine seasoning sediment will settle on the bottom of the mug, so stir occasionally while sipping or simply discard the sediment after consuming the broth.

- To prepare an instant chikun broth for soups and stews, use 1 level teaspoon of bouillon powder (more or less to taste) for each cup of simmering water. To replace Chikun Simmering Broth, add 4 tablespoons (¼ cup) bouillon powder to 12 cups simmering water. Add additional herbs and spices as desired to accommodate specific regional cuisines. Season the prepared broth with salt to taste.

- To clarify large quantities of broth, let the prepared broth cool to room temperature and then pour into a sealable container, discarding any seasoning sediment that has settled on the bottom of the cooking pot. Refrigerate for 8 to 12 hours to allow any microfine seasoning sediment to further settle on the bottom of the container. Decant the clear portion of broth and use in recipes as needed.

Better Butter

Better Butter is a superior tasting, palm oil-free alternative to dairy butter and commercial margarine. This recipe produces a semihard butter that looks, tastes, and melts like dairy butter and can be used in any recipe, including baking, just as you would use dairy butter or margarine. Better Butter will brown and burn when exposed to high heat and therefore should not be used for high-heat cooking; it works best with low to medium heat. The best kitchen appliance for emulsifying the ingredients is an immersion blender.

1 cup refined (not virgin) **coconut oil**, melted

⅓ cup neutral **vegetable oil**

⅔ cup plain **soymilk** or **almond milk**

4 teaspoons **liquid lecithin**, or 8 teaspoons **lecithin powder**

1 teaspoon **organic sugar**

1 teaspoon **nutritional yeast flakes**

½ teaspoon **lactic acid powder**, or 2 teaspoons **apple cider vinegar**

¾ teaspoon **sea salt** (omit for sweet butter)

½ teaspoon **guar gum** or **xanthan gum**

Have ready a 2-cup food storage container with a lid in which to store the butter. If you prefer, the butter can be shaped in a flexible silicone form, or divided into several forms, and released after it hardens.

Pour the coconut oil into a 2-cup measuring cup or other suitable container with a pouring lip. Add the vegetable oil and set aside.

Put the soymilk, lecithin, sugar, nutritional yeast, lactic acid powder, salt, and guar gum in a 4-cup glass measuring cup or heavy glass or ceramic bowl. Insert an immersion blender and process the mixture for 15 seconds. With the immersion blender running on high speed, slowly pour the oil mixture into the blending cup or bowl. Move the blender up and down and side to side as you add the oil mixture. Continue blending until the mixture is emulsified and thick. Transfer to the 2-cup storage container.

If soymilk was used as a base, cover the container and refrigerate the butter until solid (if you're using one or several silicone molds, cover with plastic wrap).

If almond milk was used as a base, cover and freeze the butter until solid (if you're using one or several silicone molds, cover with plastic wrap). Once the butter is frozen, put it in the refrigerator and let it thaw before using.

Alternatively, the butter can be stored in the freezer for up to 3 months. To release the butter from a form, wiggle the sides a bit to loosen the butter and then press it out onto a plate.

Seasoned Butter

Seasoned butter is a blend of nondairy butter or margarine and specially selected herbs and spices. It's wonderful for adding a flavorful crust to pan-seared meat analogues. It's also excellent for topping potatoes, corn on the cob, cooked grains, and cooked vegetables.

½ cup **nondairy butter** or **margarine**, softened to room temperature

1 tablespoon freshly squeezed **lemon juice**

2 teaspoons minced **fresh herbs** of choice (optional)

1 teaspoon **Worcestershire Sauce** (page 182) or commercial vegan equivalent

½ teaspoon **onion powder**

½ teaspoon **garlic powder**

¼ teaspoon coarsely ground **black pepper**

¼ teaspoon **paprika**

¼ teaspoon **sea salt** or **kosher salt**

Put all the ingredients in a small bowl and mash together with a fork until evenly combined. Transfer to a covered container and refrigerate until ready to use.

No-Eggy Mayo

This is my signature recipe for producing an egg-free mayonnaise that rivals egg-based mayonnaise both in flavor and texture. It's also much less expensive than commercial vegan mayonnaise. An immersion blender makes this a nearly foolproof method of preparation. Be sure to read the tips that follow.

1½ cups neutral **vegetable oil**

½ cup plain **soymilk**, chilled

1 tablespoon plus 1 teaspoon freshly squeezed **lemon juice**

2 teaspoons **organic sugar**

1 teaspoon **apple cider vinegar**

1 teaspoon **dry mustard**

1 teaspoon **fine sea salt** or **kosher salt**

¼ ground **white pepper**

Pinch **sweet paprika** or **cayenne**

Measure the oil into a liquid measuring cup (ideally it should have a lip for pouring). Set aside.

Put the soymilk, lemon juice, sugar, vinegar, dry mustard, salt, white pepper, and paprika in a 4-cup glass measuring cup or heavy glass or ceramic bowl. Insert an immersion blender and process for 10 seconds.

With the immersion blender running on high speed, pour the oil in a slow but steady stream into the cup or bowl. Move the blender up and down and side to side as you add the oil (you can stop blending to rest your arm and hand as long as you stop pouring the oil; resume when you're ready). Continue blending until all the oil is incorporated and the mixture is emulsified and very thick. Transfer to a glass jar or plastic storage container and refrigerate.

Tips from Chef Skye

- Do not substitute any other type of plant milk. Only soymilk will properly emulsify.

- Do not omit the dry mustard. It not only adds flavor but is also a natural emulsifier due to its high content of mucilage, which coats the droplets of oil. It is essential to the success of this recipe.

- This recipe can easily be cut in half if you just need 1 cup of mayonnaise.

Soy Cream

Soy cream works beautifully in delicate sauces, as it will not cause them to become too thick. It has a silky-smooth texture with no discernible grit and is very quick and easy to prepare. Light Cashew Cream (page 189) can be used as an alternative to Soy Cream for cooked sauces when additional thickening is acceptable or desired.

1½ cups plain **soymilk**, at room temperature
½ cup refined (not virgin) **coconut oil**, melted
¼ teaspoon **sea salt**

Pour the soymilk into a blender. Put the lid in place but remove the center insert. Begin blending on low speed, gradually increasing to high speed (if the milk is splashing too much in the blender jar, decrease the speed slightly). Slowly pour in the coconut oil through the opening in the lid. Continue to process for 10 seconds after the oil has been incorporated to ensure homogenization.

Transfer the cream to a sealable container and refrigerate until well chilled. The cream will thicken to the proper texture during refrigeration. Shake well before using and consume within 10 days.

Tips from Chef Skye

- Do not substitute any other type of plant milk. Only soymilk will properly emulsify.
- The soymilk must be at room temperature to emulsify properly with the coconut oil. If necessary, gently warm the milk in a saucepan over low heat. If cold soymilk is used, the coconut oil will congeal when it comes into contact with the cold liquid and disrupt the emulsification process.

Instant Sour Cream

This easy-to-make nondairy sour cream is my smoothest and creamiest recipe to date for uncultured sour cream. Please note that there is no alternative to using soymilk or lactic acid in this recipe. Thickening is dependent upon the curdling action of soymilk when lactic acid is introduced. Other plant milks will not react to the acid in the same manner and fruit acids (such as lemon juice or vinegar) will not yield the same flavor as lactic acid.

¾ cup refined (not virgin) **coconut oil**, melted

2 teaspoons **lactic acid powder**

1¼ cups plain **soymilk**, at room temperature

½ teaspoon **guar gum** or **xanthan gum**

¼ teaspoon **fine sea salt** or **kosher salt**

Measure the melted coconut oil and set aside. Measure the lactic acid, put it in a small dish, and set aside.

Put the soymilk, guar gum, and salt in a high-powered blender. Put the lid in place but remove the center insert. Process on high speed. With the blender running, add the coconut oil in a slow but steady stream through the opening in the lid. Continue to process for 15 seconds. Add the lactic acid powder all at once through the opening in the lid and process no more than 5 seconds. Turn off the blender.

Transfer the sour cream to an airtight container, seal, and refrigerate until chilled and further thickened. Stir vigorously before using. Consume within 10 days.

CULTURED SOUR CREAM: Replace ¼ cup of the soymilk with ¼ cup strained plain soy yogurt. Decrease the lactic acid powder to 1½ teaspoons and omit the guar gum. Simply the best!

Light Cashew Cream

ight Cashew Cream thickens naturally when heated. It works well as a dairy cream substitute and as an alternative to Soy Cream (page 187) in delicate cooked sauces for meat analogues.

½ cup (2½ ounces) **raw cashews**
1¾ cups **water**
¼ teaspoon **sea salt** or **kosher salt**

Rinse the cashews to remove any dust or debris, drain thoroughly, and put them in a high-powered blender. Add the water and salt and process on high speed for 2 minutes.

Transfer to a sealable container and refrigerate. Shake well before using and consume within 5 days.

Quick Buttermilk

his buttermilk has a tangy, refreshing flavor. Soymilk is essential since it thickens in the presence of lactic acid, which adds body to the buttermilk. It's excellent to use when breading or making a batter for fried chikun or for any baking purpose. It's superb for salad dressings and dips too.

1 cup plain **soymilk**
¾ teaspoon **lactic acid powder**
¼ teaspoon **sea salt** or **kosher salt**

Put all the ingredients in a storage container with a lid. Seal the container, shake well, and refrigerate until the buttermilk is thoroughly chilled before using. Stored in the refrigerator, Quick Buttermilk will keep for 2 weeks.

Buttermilk Ranch Dressing

A creamy buttermilk dressing flavored with chives and dill. Use it to dress salads or as a dip.

1 cup **No-Eggy Mayo** (page 186) or commercial vegan mayonnaise

½ cup **Quick Buttermilk** (page 189)

1 teaspoon **Dijon mustard**

½ teaspoon **onion powder**

½ teaspoon **Worcestershire Sauce** (page 182) or commercial vegan equivalent

½ teaspoon **fine sea salt** or **kosher salt**

½ teaspoon coarsely ground **black pepper**

¼ teaspoon **garlic powder**

1 tablespoon minced **fresh chives**, or 1 teaspoon **dried chives**

1 tablespoon finely chopped **fresh parsley**, or 1 teaspoon **dried parsley**

1½ teaspoons finely chopped **fresh dill**, or ½ teaspoon **dried dill weed**

Put the mayo, buttermilk, mustard, onion powder, Worcestershire Sauce, salt, pepper, and garlic powder in a small bowl and whisk until smooth. Alternatively, put the ingredients in a shaker cup with a tight-fitting lid and shake until smooth. Season with additional salt and pepper to taste. Thin with additional buttermilk if desired. Stir in the chives, parsley, and dill.

Pour into a sealable container (or store in the shaker cup). Seal tightly and refrigerate for several hours before serving to allow the flavors to blend. Stored in the refrigerator, Buttermilk Ranch Dressing will keep for 10 days.

Index

Page references for sidebars and recipe names appear in *italics*.

About the Author

I n the late summer of 2010, Skye Michael Conroy took PETA's thirty-day pledge to adhere to a vegan diet and never turned back. Further influenced by the documentary *Earthlings,* the practice of nonviolence and non-exploitation of sentient beings became an intrinsic part of his spiritual path as well as his philosophical beliefs. As he experimented with plant-based cooking, his journey as a vegan chef unfolded.

What originated as a hobby culminated in a series of self-published cookbooks and evolved as he began studying the culinary arts in depth. Chef Skye attended Rouxbe Cooking School under the direction of renowned plant-based chef Chad Sarno and received his Plant-Based Professional Certificate in 2014.

While plant-based cooking and food science are his primary passions, he's also an avid gardener and landscaper. Originally from Southern California, Chef Skye now resides in the northern Midwest with his partner, thirteen rescued cats, and one rabbit. Visit him at thegentlechef.com.

BPC

books that educate, inspire, and empower

To find your favorite books on plant-based cooking and nutrition,
raw-foods cuisine, and healthy living, visit:

BookPubCo.com

Teff Love

Kittee Berns

$21.95 • 978-1-57067-311-5

Becoming Vegan: Express Edition

Brenda Davis, RD & Vesanto Melina, MS, RD

$22.95 • 978-1-57067-295-8

Artisan Vegan Cheese

Miyoko Schinner

$21.95 • 978-1-57067-283-5

Eat Like You Give a Damn

Michelle Schwegmann & Josh Hooten

$24.95 • 978-1-57067-313-9

Purchase these titles from your favorite book source or buy them directly from:
BPC • PO Box 99 • Summertown, TN 38483 • 1-888-260-8458

Free shipping and handling on all orders